S0-ADH-931

THE SYSTEM OF THOMAS AQUINAS

THE SYSTEM OF THOMAS AQUINAS

(Formerly Titled: Mediaeval Philosophy
Illustrated from the System of Thomas Aquinas)

By

MAURICE DE WULF

DOVER PUBLICATIONS, INC.
NEW YORK

This new Dover edition first published in 1959 is an unabridged and unaltered republication of the work first published in 1922 under the title *Mediaeval Philosophy Illustrated from the System of Thomas Aquinas.*

Manufactured in the United States of America

Dover Publications, Inc.
180 Varick Street
New York 14, N. Y.

TO MY FRIEND

JAMES HAUGHTON WOODS

MY special thanks are due to my former pupil Dr. Ernest Messenger, now professor of philosophy at Ware (England), who has translated from the French the manuscript of this book.

Subsequently, I have modified profoundly the ideas of this original version; and in this work Mr. R. Demos and Mr. R. M. Eaton have very kindly assisted me, as they have also in the correcting of the proofs. I take pleasure in expressing to them my gratitude.

M. D. W.

CONTENTS

THE SYSTEM OF THOMAS AQUINAS

CHAPTER I

INTRODUCTION

I. The place of Thomism in Mediaeval Philosophy.
II. Plan and Method.

I. *The place of Thomism in Mediaeval Philosophy.* Some years ago I made a circuit of the French Cathedrals under the guidance of a friend who is an archaeologist. "We shall visit first," said he, "the cathedral of Amiens, for it is the prototype of many other churches, and it is easier there than elsewhere to study the vaulting, pointing, pillars, buttresses, and all the other elements which enter into the grammar of Gothic architecture. After Amiens, we shall visit in turn Beauvais, Rheims, Paris, Laon, and Chartres. But, in doing so, we shall constantly refer back to what we have seen at Amiens, in order to point out resemblances or differences."

This wise procedure, to the happy results of which I can testify, can be applied with equal advantage in the study of the scholastic philosophy of the thirteenth century, a system of thought contemporaneous and intimately connected with the great productions of Gothic architecture. And just as in order to understand the structural methods of the mediaeval architects it is well to take some one building as a type or model, so also, in the study of the system of ideas known as scholastic philosophy, we could not adopt a better pedagogic method than the consideration of the typical expression of the system, as presented to us by Thomas Aquinas in the years about 1260–70. This procedure will enable those who wish to examine, by way of comparison, the solutions to the same problems given by Bonaventure, Duns Scotus, William of Occam, and others.

There is another consideration which explains why, in our brief outline of scholastic philosophy, we treat principally of Thomism. The scholastic philosophy of the thirteenth century is a common and impersonal patrimony which is the product of many generations; and this patrimonial character — a trait which is found also in the architecture, sculpture, painting, literature, legal studies, and the theology of this period — enables us thus to condense into the study of one single giant of thought that which really belongs to the whole period in question. Aquinas is the most striking representative of this common philosophy (*sententia communis*). He is the complement of the past even more than the beginning of a new trend of thought. He was not the discoverer of all the doctrines which go to make up his philosophical system. As a matter of fact, he introduced comparatively few new ideas; but no one has rivaled him in coördinating doctrines borrowed from his predecessors and in systematizing the philosophical notions of the world and of human life.[1] He embodied in philosophy the unifying tendencies which were evident everywhere in the civilization of the thirteenth century. Aquinas belonged to an epoch of great ideas and great achievements, when men fancied that they had at last realized a permanent and durable civilization — in fact, a position of stable equilibrium, completely satisfying St. Augustine's definition of peace: *Pax est tranquillitas ordinis.* Peace is the tranquillity of order.

[1] See our *Histoire de la philosophie médiévale*, 4th edition, 1912. A fifth French edition is in preparation.

The pedagogical aim which we have before us in this little book forces us to limit ourselves to the consideration of the great and central doctrines of Thomism, and to leave aside the innumerable applications of those doctrines which may be found scattered up and down the extensive works of Thomas Aquinas.

Nor shall we be able to deal with the relations between Thomism and the civilization with which it was contemporaneous. We have treated this subject in a recent book, *Civilization and Philosophy in the Middle Ages*[1] to which we refer the reader. Some of the philosophical theories developed in that work are taken up again here, but from another point of view, in such a way that the two books supplement one another.

There is yet another point to which we must call attention: We are concerned only with scholastic Philosophy, and not with scholastic Theology, or with Catholic dogma. It is no doubt true that there were close relations between scholastic Philosophy and Theology in the thirteenth century. Philosophy derived its inspiration from Theology in a certain sense; for it was planted in a civilization of which religion was a powerful element. But this philosophy is religious only in the sense in which one can apply the term to art, politics, and domestic, social and economic institutions generally. The philosophical work of Thomas Aquinas forms with his theological work a diptych, of which the two wings complete or rather supplement each other, yet each retains its own independent significance. The same is true of the *Divine Comedy* of Dante; it is at once an artistic poem which "heaven and earth combine to form," and a religious book "which aims

[1] Princeton University Press, 1922, pp. viii, 316.

at delivering mortals from their state of misery and conducting them to eternal happiness." Again, the same applies to a Gothic cathedral, which is an artistic marvel and also a house of prayer. It is quite possible to leave aside the religious connections of scholastic philosophy with Catholicism and consider its religious problems only in so far as they enter into a conception of the world and of human life, based upon pure reason.

Only a conscientious study of the Aquinas of history can enable a person to judge to what extent the philosophical doctrines of Thomism retain their value to-day. It alone can give us the means of sifting the theories which are true and alive from those which are false or superannuated. By this means we shall be able to distinguish those doctrines which had a meaning for the Middle Ages only, and are entirely bound up with a bygone civilization, from those other doctrines which can be transplanted into our own times and continue to satisfy that need of the ideal which exists forever in the human soul.

II. *Plan and Method.* It remains to notice the plan which we shall follow. In our survey of scholastic philosophy, we shall remain faithful to a classification which the Schoolmen themselves adopted, and which will be indicated and justified at the end of this book (XVIII). At the same time this classification will explain our own method.

The first chapters will be devoted to the study of human activities — conscious and unconscious — and principally to the study of knowing and willing (II–VII). We shall then consider certain general views concerning the constitution of material things still with special reference to man (VIII–X). Another chapter will be devoted to the study of God (XI). This first group of doctrines corresponds to what the Schoolmen call the *theoretical* portion of their philosophy.

The chapters on *practical* philosophy will treat of the fundamental doctrines concerning individual morality (XII–XIV), social philosophy (XV), the logic of the sciences (XVI), and esthetics (XVII). A general summing up will bring out the principal characteristics which belong to this doctrinal structure as a whole (XIX).

The philosophical terminology we employ in this book is that of Aquinas and his contemporaries. But we shall use it only when necessary, and we have tried throughout to give for all the technical terms, so far as possible, a modern equivalent, or at least, to show how their usage differs from that of to-day. It is impossible, however, to avoid some important technical terms. Every science has its own vocabulary — chemistry, mathematics are cases in point. So it is not surprising that philosophy should have its own. I do not believe it possible to follow the advice of Locke, that philosophy, when speaking to the public, should use the language of the ordinary man. Locke himself failed to practice what he preached. All that one can require is an explanation in common terms of the technical language used.

Few quotations will be found in the present work, since we propose to publish a separate volume of selected readings, taken from the principal writings of Aquinas. All books cited in footnotes are by him, unless otherwise specified.

CHAPTER II

DIFFERENT KINDS OF KNOWLEDGE

I. Central position of the theory of knowledge.
II. Two irreductible types of knowledge. Knowledge of particular objects and its forms.
III. Abstract and general knowledge.
IV. Several forms of intellectual knowledge. Idea, judgment, reasoning.
V. The wide field of consciousness.

I. *Central position of the theory of knowledge.* The Schoolmen of the thirteenth century paid special attention to the functions of knowing and willing. They regarded these as the peculiar and privileged possession of the human race, situated as it is at the boundary where matter and spirit meet. For, the dignity of man results from a certain way of knowing which is peculiar to him, and which is called intelligence. This we must define more closely, in order to understand in what sense scholasticism can be described as an intellectualist system of philosophy.

What is knowing? An object is known when it is present in a certain way in the knowing consciousness. When I see a stone lying in a road, the stone is *present in* me, but not indeed in the material way in which it is present outside of me in the external world. For it is perfectly clear that "the stone is not in me so far as its own peculiar existence is concerned." [1] In the same way, when I grasp mentally the constituent nature of the molecule of water, and the law which governs its decomposition (H_2O), the material existence of the mole-

[1] *De Veritate*, q. 23, art. 1. *In lib. III de anima*, I, q. 9.

cule does not in any way enter into or form part of me; but there is produced in me a kind of reflection of a non-ego. The privilege of a being which knows consists precisely in this ability of being enriched by something which belongs to something else. "Knowing beings are differentiated from non-knowing beings by this characteristic: non-knowing beings have only their own reality, but knowing beings are capable of possessing also the reality of something else. For in the knowing being there is a presence of the thing known produced by this thing." [1]

In what does this presence or reflection of the object in me consist? The Schoolmen do not pretend to fathom the mystery of knowledge; their explanation is a mere analysis of facts revealed by introspection.

Knowing, they observe, is a particular kind of being, a modification, or a vital action of the knowing subject. "The thing known is present in the knowing subject according to the mode of being of the knowing subject"; it bears its mark. "All knowledge results from a similitude of the thing known in the subject knowing." [2] These two quotations, which were common sayings, sum up well the views of the thirteenth century psychologists. In consequence, knowledge does not result merely from the thing; but rather, the thing known and the subject knowing coöperate in the production of the phenomenon. This intervention of the knowing subject shows us why scholasticism rejected 'naïve realism,' which disregards the action of the knowing subject, and considers the object known as projected in our

[1] *Summa Theol.*, I[a], q. 14, art. 1.

[2] Cognitum est in cognoscente secundum modum cognoscentis. Omnis cognitio fit secundum similitudinem cogniti in cognoscente.

minds like an image in a lifeless and passive mirror. On the other hand, since there is an activity of the thing known upon the knowing subject, our representations of reality will be to some extent faithful and correspond to that reality.

II. *Two irreducible types of knowledge. Knowledge of particular objects and its forms.* It is of great importance to note that scholasticism distinguishes between two quite different kinds of knowledge: sense knowledge, and intellectual knowledge. In the case of the first — the perception by sight of an oak tree, for instance — everything that I grasp is particularized or individualized, and intimately bound up with conditions of space and time. What I see is *this* oak tree, with a trunk of *this* particular form, with a bark of *this* degree of roughness, with *these* particular branches and *these* leaves, in *this* particular spot in the forest, and which came from a particular acorn at a particular moment of time. If I touch the tree with my hand, the resistance which I encounter is *this* resistance, just as the sound which I hear in striking the bark is *this* sound. Our external senses (sight, hearing, smell, taste, touch) put us in contact either with something which is a proper and peculiar object of *one* sense and which each sense perceives to the exclusion of all the others (*sensibile proprium*), for instance, color in the case of sight; or else the common object (*sensibile commune*) of more than one sense, for instance, shape in the case of sight and touch. But in every case the reality perceived by sense is always endowed with individuality.

The same is true of those sensations which are called internal, and which originate, in the scholastic system of classification, from sense-memory (*a*), from sense-consciousness (*b*), from instinct (*c*), or from imagination (*d*). These are simply so many labels attached to psychological facts which have been duly observed and noted. A few examples will make this clear.

(*a*) Sense-memory. When I have ceased to look at the oak tree, there remains in me an after-image, which is said to be 'preserved' in memory, since I am able to 'reproduce' it. We thus possess in ourselves a storehouse of after-images received through the senses,[1] which can be reproduced either spontaneously, or else at the command of the will. It is clear that these vestiges of past sensations, retained and reproduced in this way, are individualized just as the original sensation. If I picture to myself an oak tree, it will always be a picture of *one* individual oak tree. In the same way, when we realize that a sense perception, or a conscious act of our physiological life, has a certain duration, or takes place after another activity, this realization, which itself involves sense-memory, is once more individual and singular, and presents us with *this* particular time.[2] The recognition of past time involves reference to particular psychological events, following each other.

(*b*) Sense-consciousness. Moreover, when I look at an oak tree, something in me tells me that I see. I am aware that I am seeing. My sense perception is followed by 'sense-consciousness,' and the content of this sense-consciousness is particularized. Again, the complex sense cognition of this oak as an object is the result of the coördination of many sense perceptions coming

[1] Thesaurus quidam formarum per sensum acceptarum *De Veritate*, q. 10, art. 2.

[2] It is quite different from the abstract notion of time in general. That belongs to intellectual knowledge. (Cf. VIII, 4.)

from different senses: the height of the tree, the roughness of its bark, the hollow sound which its trunk gives when struck. There is reason to attribute to the higher animals and to man a central sense,[1] which combines the external sense perceptions, compares them, and discriminates between them. But in this case also, the result of these operations is individualized, and if we compare for instance two complex sense perceptions of oak trees, each is itself and not the other.

(*c*) Instinct. We can apply the same to the way in which we recognize that a certain situation is dangerous for us or otherwise. We possess a discriminating power which estimates certain concrete connections between things. We naturally flee from fire, and a shipwrecked man clutches instinctively at a plank, much in the same way as a lamb looks upon a wolf as dangerous, and a bird considers a particular branch of a tree as a suitable resting-place for its nest. This act of sense knowledge always relates to a particular, concrete situation.[2]

(*d*) Imagination. Again, the constructive imagination, which takes the materials supplied by sense-memory and combines them into all sorts of fantastic images — when I imagine, for instance, oak trees as high as mountains, and monstrosities half lion half man — deals with what is particularized. What modern psychologists might call a composite image is to the Schoolmen simply a particular image, made up of characters derived from other particular images.

[1] Called *sensus communis,* which is quite different from what is called to-day common sense. *De potentiis animae,* cap. IV.

[2] In the case of the animals, it is the result of a *mere instinct* by which they appreciate certain things as harmful, and others as suitable (naturalis aestimatio ad cognoscendum nocivum et conveniens). Man, on the other hand, is guided by his reason "which juxtaposes things in order to compare them" (*Summa Theol.,* I^a, q. 78, art. 4).

III. *Abstract and general knowledge.* Introspection shows us that we possess another kind of knowledge with characteristics quite different from those we have found in sense knowledge. Intellectual knowledge, instead of being concrete and particularized, is abstract and general. Let us consider this twofold character.

The act of vision of an oak tree, localized in a particular spot, is spontaneously accompanied by notions such as 'height,' 'cylindrical form,' 'local motion,' 'color,' 'vital activity,' 'cell,' 'matter,' 'being.' These notions are indeed derived from this oak tree, but the aspects of reality which we grasp by them are no longer bound up with this particular individual: they reveal to me the *whatness* or essence (*essentia, quidditas*),[1] or in what height, local motion, life activity, combustion, etc., consist. We confine our attention to certain elements of the thing under consideration, *shutting out all the other elements, and stripping them of all particularizing determinations.* Abstraction consists precisely in this function and in nothing else. In what *height* consists is considered apart from everything else, and this selected aspect of reality is no longer related to this oak tree. So that the term abstraction has its etymological meaning (*trahere ab*, to select from, to draw from; abstraction is sometimes called *praecisio mentalis*). I possess a treasure-house of abstract notions which relate to all kinds and classes of reality.

It is precisely *because* this representative content, or object [2] of thought (*id quod menti objicitur*), is no longer bound up entirely with the sight of any particular oak

[1] Quidditas, quod quid est (τὸ τί ἦν εἶναι of Aristotle).

[2] Object is taken as content of knowledge, as something *before* the mind: id quod menti objicitur.

tree, or of a particular human being, etc., that it is seen upon reflection to be applicable to an indefinite number of beings which move, which are cylindrical in form, which manifest vital activities, which are material in nature, etc. This applicability is indefinite — it is 'universal' or general, and extends to possible realities as well as existent ones. Universality, therefore, follows upon abstraction, as Thomas remarks.

An *abstract* notion of mankind seizes *what* mankind is, as distinct from the whatness of an elephant or a particle of radium. A *universal* or general notion of mankind implies that such a reality is represented as being able to belong to an endless multitude of men. An abstract notion is thus not necessarily universal, but it may become so. If we bear this in mind, we shall be able to understand better the scholastic solution of the problem of Universals.

We said above that there is no such thing as a general image. Here we say that there is such a thing as a general idea — in fact, that all ideas are general. There is no contradiction here. But those who are unaccustomed to introspection are often unconscious of the vital distinction between image and idea which underlies our two statements. The average man labels his mental content as 'images' and 'ideas' indiscriminately. Yet reflection will show that they are quite different, and that the one is general while the other is not. This will be made clear from the example of a geometrical theorem — for instance, that the angles of a triangle are together equal to two right angles. We go on at once to picture a triangle, and we say, "Let ABC be a triangle," and so on. But this image of a triangle is a particular one, whereas our reasoning applies to any and all triangles, existent or only possible. It is thus obvious that the idea or concept triangle is abstract and general, whereas the image is not. The image is here simply a help to our mental consideration and reflection.

The knowledge of reality by means of abstract and universal notions is quite distinct from the particular, individualized knowledge of the external and internal senses. The Schoolmen emphasize this difference by attributing abstract knowledge to the intelligence (*intellectus*) or reason (*ratio*). The prominent place occupied in scholasticism by this doctrine of abstract and general knowledge, which we may describe as 'Psychological Spiritualism' or better still as Intellectualism, gives the system a definite place in the brilliant group to which belong Plato, Aristotle, Augustine, Plotinus, and in later times, Descartes, Leibnitz, Kant.

Abstraction is the privilege and the distinctive act of man. It is likewise the central activity of our conscious life. The intellectualism, which results from this theory, has an influence over all the branches of philosophy, and we shall see that the rights of human reason are proclaimed and defended at every stage of thought.

IV. *Several forms of intellectual knowledge. Idea, judgment, reasoning.* Just as the sense knowledge of particular things has many forms, so also intellectual or abstract knowledge presents several stages — simple apprehension, judgment, and reasoning. They all are fundamentally abstract knowledge, i. e., an understanding of *what* something is, *apart from the particularizing conditions in which it exists*, or is capable of existing, outside the mind. Which are the psychological features of these three forms of thought?

In simple apprehension or concept or idea, the mind considers what a thing is, without affirming or denying anything about it. Example: triangle, square, whole, part.

The act of judgment consists in realizing that the content of two ideas — or two objects present to the mind — are in mutual agreement or disagreement. Example: the triangle *is* a surface; the triangle *is not* a sphere.

The abstract character which belongs to all our thoughts explains why the mind must make judgments, i. e., affirm this mutual agreement or disagreement. Why is it that we say, "the sum of the angles of a triangle *is* equal to two right angles," "wine *is* changing into vinegar when exposed to the air"? Why are we not content simply to form the ideas 'triangle', 'wine'? The answer lies in the richness of reality,[1] and in the weakness of our minds. We are incapable of grasping by one single insight, or by one adequate intuition, all that there is in a real being. Only the penetrating eyes of God can exhaust the intelligibility of things by a single intuition, as Leibnitz says, and read in a blade of grass the network of relations which constitutes the history of the universe. Only God is able

> To see a World in a grain of sand,
> And a Heaven in a wild flower,
> Hold Infinity in the palm of your hand,
> And Eternity in an hour.[2]

[1] By *reality* we mean something which is not a mere product of the mind, — as opposed to the unreal or fictitious. The real is either existent, e. g., the sun, or else a possible thing, e. g., a triangle. The object of the idea 'darkness' is on the contrary unreal.

[2] William Blake, "Auguries of Innocence," *Works*, Oxford Edition, 1914, p. 171.

Our human mind, on the contrary, has to grasp reality piecemeal, and by partial aspects, or partial abstractions. We hunt and stalk reality, in the expressive language of the Schoolmen (*venari*), but never completely capture it. We discover in a triangle its properties and relations, we seize the activities, reactions of water. Then, after this mental dissection, we refer back to the thing we are studying — now become the subject of a judgment — each and all of the aspects discovered during our patient investigations. These several aspects correspond to several predicates of our judgments. Thus we say S *is* P, " water freezes at 0°C., it is composed of H_2O, it boils at 100°C., etc." The mind unites things, after it has decomposed them, it makes a synthesis, and thus presents us with a complex object of knowledge. This explains why the notion which a chemist has of water is much richer in content than that of an ordinary person. Likewise, in a fragment of a Greek statue, the common man only knows superficial realities: marble, hardness, whiteness, etc., whilst the archaeologist places the whole statue in the history of art and as a part of an entire civilization. Judgment, then, which unites or separates (*compositio*, *divisio* are the scholastic terms), begins and ends with abstraction.

It follows from this that any of the aspects of an object (S) may become the predicate (P) of a judgment — not only those aspects which are qualities or attributes, but also activities displayed, state of existence, a relation, a situation in time or space. For example, the horse (S) is drawing a carriage, is sick, has more endurance than a mule, appeared in prehistoric time, in Northern Europe (P). Each of these aspects, which plays a part in making up the richness of the real object S is referred back to S by the mechanism of judgment through the use of the copula *is*. The verb *is* does not indicate an inherence in the subject of any of those aspects, but the mental agreement of the subject and the predicate.[1]

The same remarks apply to the process of reasoning, which is simply the production of a new judgment by means of two others, and whose final aim is to enrich the store of abstract knowledge about the special material (such as plants, human acts, numbers, etc.) upon which a special science turns its attention.

V. *The wide field of consciousness.* Just as we become witnesses of our sense perceptions, so also consciousness accompanies the exercise of our ideas, our judgments, our reasonings.

Not only is it the case that each act of thought is spontaneously accompanied by a sort of intuition of what is happening in us, but in addition, by an effort of will, we can turn back to this act of thought and investigate either the operation itself as a modification of the ego (psychological consciousness), or else as a mental content, a representation of something (objective consciousness). This is brought about by a sort of twisting or turning back upon ourselves, which we cannot better describe than as reflection (*re-flect*: to bend back). When I reflect upon the idea of local displacement, of life, or on any other object of thought, it is this object itself which I encounter in the first place, and which I make the material of my inquiries (objective consciousness). The subjective operation which this inquiry in-

[1] Russell has on this point misunderstood the 'traditional' logic. *Our Knowledge of the External World*, p. 45 (London, 1914).

volves, the relation of the object to myself, or the internal mechanism of my operation (subjective consciousness) all call for a further concentration, which is much more complicated and difficult. This agrees with and confirms the Thomistic doctrine that knowledge, whether spontaneous or reflective, puts us in presence of 'something' which is not merely my own activity, as idealists maintain.

Man alone possesses this privilege of reflecting, or of bending his consciousness upon itself, for reflection is peculiar to spiritual beings. Animals do not reflect; even the human senses cannot do so, and that is the reason why our senses are incapable of correcting by themselves alone the illusions or errors of which they may be victims. Without reflection, I should have no means of knowing that a stick plunged in the water is really straight, in spite of appearances to the contrary. I should remain forever the dupe of sense appearances, for these continue to exist even while reflection is correcting them (VI, 5).

Consciousness accompanies not only our sense perceptions and thoughts, but also certain functions of our physiological life, our appetites, volitions, and sentiments or affections. Further, not only does it accompany the *exercise* of our activities, but it attains in a more obscure way the *ego*, which exists in these activities. "I think, therefore I exist," is an intuition, which St. Augustine and Thomas Aquinas formulated long before Descartes.

CHAPTER III

HOW OUR KNOWLEDGE IS FORMED

I. Origin of sensations. Psychical and physical aspects.
II. Origin of intellectual knowledge.

I. *Origin of sensations. Psychical and physical aspects.* There are still two important questions concerning the different kinds of knowledge which consciousness reveals to us: how they are formed and what is their value. These two questions are quite distinct, and form the subject of the following chapters. Here we shall discuss how knowledge, whether sensuous or intellectual, comes into existence.

As soon as a child awakens to life, his external senses bring him into contact with something other than his consciousness: the color, taste, shape, resistance, temperature, etc., of material things. Throughout life, sensations continue to play this principal rôle. Now, according to the Schoolmen, a sensation necessitates an influx of a particular object known and the reaction of the subject knowing. Let us take the sight of an oak tree as an example. The sense or psychic power of sight does not derive *from itself* the content of its act of vision. An impulse coming from outside and received by me is an indispensable factor, without which an act of sight would be impossible But as soon as that impulse coming from the oak tree is received in me, I react to the stimulus, and this vital reaction completes the sense perception. The whole phenomenon is imprinted from outside, and exhibited from inside; it has a passive aspect and an active one. The Schoolmen employed the terms *species impressa* and *expressa* to signify these two aspects (impression and reaction) relating sensuous knowledge to the object known or to the subject knowing.

Thomas insists that this sense impression "is not known directly" (*id quod cognoscitur*). What is present to sense consciousness, what we attain to, is the thing itself — the oak tree. The impression which it produces in me is known only by a reasoning process. We realize *why* an impulse coming from the external object is the necessary condition by which we know (*id quo cognoscitur*) — just as nervous activity is needed in sense perceptions and is not perceived by consciousness. Analyzing what actually *is*, we conclude that something else *must be*.

The phenomenon, which we have just been considering, is wholly *psychical*, since it takes place completely *in us*, and is of a cognitive kind.[1] Therefore, the problem of the transmitting medium of sensations is quite distinct from it. By what medium is it that the oak tree, situated a distance of ten yards, say, from my eye, affects my organism? A few Schoolmen, such as Henry of Ghent, confounded this problem with the previous one. Thomas Aquinas and Duns Scotus, on the contrary, carefully distinguished them. The transmission of the physical action of external objects through the intervening air or water is treated in general in accordance with their notions of physics, which we need not enter into here.[2]

[1] The analysis given above deals only with external sensations. In the case of internal sensations, it is the trace left by the external sensation which sets in motion the series of acts of imagination and of sense memory.

[2] Since the *species* of the Schoolmen are nothing but a vital reaction;

II. *Origin of intellectual knowledge.* There is a well-known adage of scholastic and thomist psychology, which states that we derive the content of our abstract ideas from the content of our sensations, and, by means of these, ultimately from the material universe. *Nihil est in intellectu quod prius non fuerit in sensu.* "There is nothing in the mind which was not first in the senses." Our ideas of life, strength, greatness, motion, action exercised or received, double, half, left, right, etc. — all these and a thousand others equally abstract in nature — are derived from our sense perception of the objects which surround us. We have proper and direct knowledge of the material world only. Our mind is closely united to our body, and it is in and through the corporeal bodies that we obtain our intellectual knowledge.

It follows from this that even moral ideas (justice, right, etc.) and our knowledge of spiritual beings (the mind, spirits, God) is derived from, and must be expressed in terms of the material, by means of comparison, analogy, negation, and transcendence. We have only an improper and indirect idea of what is spiritual. Although we can prove that there is such a thing as a

since the impulse of the external being (the oak tree) is psychological, it would be a misunderstanding of the scholastic doctrine to consider the *species* as particles which are detached from the body perceived, and which pass into the percipient. This false interpretation, similar to the theory of εἴδωλα of Democritus, belongs to some decadent Schoolmen of the sixteenth and seventeenth centuries. This fact explains why Leibnitz disparages the scholastic theory of the *species*. He writes, "Accidents cannot separate themselves from substances nor go about outside of them as the sensible species of the scholastics used to do." *The Monadology*, translated by R. Latta, Oxford Press, 1898, p. 129. It is important to notice that the Schoolmen of the decadence, at whom the objections of Leibnitz were aimed, misinterpreted the psychological doctrine of the thirteenth century. Latta does justice to the thirteenth century. "Leibnitz is thinking of a theory (*not* that of Thomas Aquinas)," p. 220.

spiritual being, we do not know in what it consists properly, and our feeble minds have to conceive it by applying to it the notions of being, reality, causality, etc., which have come to us through the channel of our senses.

The problem of the origin of our abstract thoughts, however, is to be solved in the same way in which it is solved for our sensations. But it is more complicated on account of a special difficulty.

Before meeting this difficulty, let us take note of the similarity which exists between the processes of sensation and of thought, and why, in the last analysis, both will be solved in the same way. This similarity consists in the initial impression coming from an external impulse, and followed by a characteristic reaction which belongs to thought as well as to sensation. For, experience and consciousness alike prove that the mind also needs to be determined or completed by the corporeal object known, and that it does not derive merely from itself the content of its ideas. A blind man has no idea of color. Left to itself, our mind would be an empty desert, or a clean slate (*tabula rasa*), with nothing written on it.[1] Here, as in the case of sensation, there is a passage from potentiality to actuality; there is an initial passive state, and there is an impression which is received (*species intelligibilis impressa*). The two horses or dollars from which I derive the abstract idea of the number 'two,' or of 'money,' 'power,' 'form,' etc., act upon my mind. And just as in the case of sensation, the mind reacts to the stimulus and answers by a vital act, by means of which the phenomenon of knowledge is completed (*species intelligibilis expressa*).

[1] *Summa Theol.*, I^a^, q. 79, art. 2.

Now we have to deal with a special difficulty which arises in the case of abstract knowledge. This difficulty appears because it is necessary to harmonize the doctrine of which we have just been speaking with a central teaching of scholastic metaphysics. We shall see later on that the universe of all Schoolmen without exception is a pluralistic one, and that each of the myriad beings of which it is composed has its own separate and independent existence (VIII, 1). Each oak tree possesses its own being, independent of all others, and this is equally true of men, animals, etc. And thence comes the difficulty: a particular individual thing, such as an oak tree, can give rise to a sensation of sight which is in turn particularized; but how can it give rise to abstract notions such as life, cylindrical form, without the particularizing conditions which belong to each *real* living, or cylindrical being? How can *this* particular living being give rise to the notion of *life* as such? How can the concrete be known abstractly?

The external object (which we here suppose to exist outside of us) cannot determine thought in the same way as it determines sensation. By itself alone it is powerless. The two horses, being particularized and individual, cannot, by means of the sensations they produce, give rise to an impression in us which gives them a mode of being different in kind and superior (abstract) to that which really belongs to them (particular, concrete). Otherwise we should have a cause producing an effect superior to itself. The less would produce the more. At this point, Scholasticism adopts an Aristotelian theory. It is *not only* the two horses or two dollars which act upon my intelligence, but the sensation of the two horses or dollars act in coöperation with and in dependence upon a special spiritual power within me, which "shines upon the sense data, and makes them capable and ready to produce a knowledge in which reality is deprived of all its concrete and individual features." This creative power is called active intellect (*intellectus agens*), and in opposition to it the mind or the intelligence in which the impression is produced, under the twofold influence of the corporeal beings and the *intellectus agens*, is called *intellectus possibilis*.

It is important to note here as in the case of sensation, that our minds grasp directly, in the two dollars, the content 'two,' 'money,' 'paper,' etc.; but in attaining these notions, we are aware neither of the spiritual power of abstracting, nor of the impression (*species impressa*) which it produces in us by the object known. It is again by a process of reasoning, which seeks for an adequate explanation of the phenomenon, that we pass from what *is* to what *must be.* This does not imply that by means of this theory we understand the whole mechanism of thought. The latter remains a mystery. In many questions we must be satisfied to know that something exists, even if we cannot penetrate its inmost nature. We ought never to ask of a theory more than it undertakes to do.

CHAPTER IV

THE DIRECTING PRINCIPLES OF KNOWLEDGE

I. General notion of the directing principles of knowledge.
II. Origin and nature of these principles.
III. Logical and real value.

I. *General notion of the directing principles of knowledge.* Our knowledge consists of judgments, connected and coördinated with one another. The progressive life of the mind moves by a regular process in which judgments are built upon other judgments, so that the judgment is the principal and central act of the mind (II, 4). Amongst these mental enunciations there are some which play a capital rôle in the life of the mind. They rule not only its psychological development, but also its epistemological and logical functioning, and therefore they deserve our special attention. We call them the directing principles of knowledge. To this class belong the principle of contradiction (a thing cannot both be and not be); the principle of identity (that which is, is; being is equal to itself); the principle of excluded middle (there is no middle term between being and non-being); the principle of sufficient reason (being is endowed with all the elements without which it could not be); the principle of totality (the whole is equal to the sum of its parts); the principle of efficient causality (non-necessary being exists by the influence of a being other than itself). There are many others. All form one long series, in close connection with the principle of contradiction, of which they all express different elementary phases or applications.

These judgments are called *principles* because they serve as a basis for other judgments: *first* or immediate principles, because it is impossible to prove them by reference to more fundamental judgments; *directing* principles (axioms or *axiomata* in the language of the Schoolmen) because they express simple relations between being, of whatever kind it may be, and certain elementary and primordial notions which are connected with being, such as 'non-being,' 'whole,' 'part,' 'commencement of existence.'

II. *Origin and nature of these principles.* We may say that experience is the *source* of these principles, in the sense that the ideas which form the subject and predicates of the judgment are derived from experience. 'Being,' 'whole,' 'commencement of existence,' 'causality,' are derived from the matter of our internal and external sensations, by way of abstraction. We may go farther and say that experience *facilitates* the enunciation of the relation between the subject and predicate. For instance, I enunciate the principle of contradiction in realizing that I cannot be in the lecture hall and in the dark room at the same time; and the principle of causality, in realizing that my arm is raised by the command of my will acting as a cause.

But it is of vital importance to note that for the Schoolmen the *bond of union* established between the subject and predicate of the first principles we are considering is based, not upon experience, but upon the content of the subject and predicate, as revealed by mere analysis. When I say A = A, this judgment results from the mere consideration of A (whatever it may be) and not from experience. Since it does not depend upon human experience, which attains only to what *actually* exists, the bond of union expressed by these principles is therefore independent of the existence of the present universe, and, in fact, of all creation. Their validity does not depend on the *condition* that something exists: it is absolute. If the universe had never existed, and there was just one intelligence besides God, this would have been capable of knowing the axioms which govern human knowledge. The idea of being, and the other primordial notions correlative to it, could be obtained by such an intelligence from its knowledge of itself, or from God, and the juxtaposition of subject and predicate is sufficient to reveal the relation between them in the case of the axioms in question.

This supposition shows that there is no contradiction between the view expressed earlier that the constituent ideas of these principles (being, non-being, totality, etc.) are abstracted by the mind from external or internal sense perceptions, and this other view that the bond uniting these contents may be grasped without the aid of experience.

By reason of these characteristics, directing principles or axioms belong to a comprehensive class of judgments which are said to be 'knowable as a result of the mere juxtaposition of the terms' subject and predicate (*propositio per se nota*) and which would be called to-day judgments of the *ideal order*.

This class of judgments is opposed to a second category, which we need not study here, but which we mention only in order to emphasize the nature of the directing principles which we are now considering. In this second category of judgments, it no longer suffices to juxtapose the terms in order to see the relation between them: we must have recourse in addition to experience (*propositio per aliud nota;* the *aliud* is experience). If I do not need to subject my judgment to the control of experience in order to know that being and non-being are mutually exclusive, this control is indispensable in the case of the judgment that water boils at 100° C.; or that men have a natural tendency to live in social groups. The second class of judgments would be known to-day as judgments of the *existential order* (XVI, 2).

Let us consider more closely the group of judgments to which our directing principles belong. It would appear at first sight that the judgment of the ideal order of the Schoolmen coincides with the 'judgment *de jure*' of Leibnitz, and the 'analytic' judgment of Kant, i.e., the judgment in which the subject includes the predicate. It is true that scholastic philosophy classifies among judgments of the ideal order these propositions, which Kant despised as mere tautologies. But Thomas Aquinas goes on to point out that there is another kind of judgments of the ideal order, knowable by the mere analysis of the subject and the predicate, and which is much more interesting. In these the predicate is *not included in* the subject, but nevertheless a clear knowledge or insight into the predicate reveals the bond which indissolubly unites it with the subject, once this subject is given. Although the predicate is not contained within the subject, there is an *exigentia*, or need, which imperiously demands the union of predicate and subject. The axioms which we are considering in this chapter all belong to this second class, except perhaps the principle of identity.

Take, for instance, the principles of contradiction and that of causality. The mere analysis of the notion of being will never reveal the notion of non-being (the negation is not implied in the affirmation), nor that of incompatibility with (the relation *with* is not implied in the notion of a thing considered in itself). But once the ideas of being and non-being are present to a mind the incompatibility of the two is forcibly evident. Or again, from the notion of 'non-necessary existence' we could never deduce that of 'actual existence in the realm of fact.' But if we juxtapose and compare the two notions, it is evident to us at once that the one is not the other, and that if a non-necessary thing is conceived as existing in point of fact we cannot explain this existence, without something other than itself. Indeed, a non-necessary thing is non-existent of itself. Hence, it cannot give to itself what it does not possess. As soon as this non-necessary being is represented as existing, it ought to be referred to some *external* influence — a causal influence — which is the sufficient reason of this existence. This is the enunciation of the principle of efficient causality: "The existence of a non-necessary being demands a cause."

III. *Logical and real value.* Since the relation which unites the terms of the directing principles is so evident that it "leaps to the eyes" as the French say (*sauter aux yeux*), independently of experience, and since these principles express the laws of being as such and of all being, there will be no difficulty in allowing that they govern all *conceivable* being. They direct and control every assertion; they rule 'universal intelligibility.' They therefore rule and guide the collection of judgments which go to make up our human sciences, and likewise the various judgments which regulate our practical life. For instance, if the principle of contradiction were to become uncertain, or doubtful, no human *affirmation* would hold good, — not even the famous dictum, "I think, therefore I exist." The assertion of my existence is not valid, if what I perceive as real can both be and not be. For this reason the principle of contradiction is called by the Schoolmen the first principle *par excellence*, and they make their own the declaration of Aristotle to the effect that a person who could not grasp this principle would not be a man, but a blockhead.

Do these principles, which apply to all conceivable beings, also govern *existent* being, in case anything is proved to exist? And if they govern the material universe as a whole, will they apply also to a world of suprasensible or spiritual beings, if such exist? These questions form part of the great epistemological problem which we must now consider.

CHAPTER V

VARIOUS ASPECTS OF THE EPISTEMOLOGICAL PROBLEM

I. Metaphysical and psychological aspects.
II. The data of the epistemological problem.

I. *Metaphysical and psychological aspects.* The Schoolmen of the thirteenth century never doubted for a moment that our faculties of knowing are capable of attaining extra-mental reality. In those dogmatic days there were no critics and adversaries such as those of later times, for whom the critical problem of knowledge occupies so large a place in philosophical speculation.

In the writings of Thomas Aquinas, and especially in the fine treatise concerning Truth (*De Veritate*), the problem of truth is considered from two distinct points of view. The first is metaphysical; the second psychological and critical.

The metaphysical doctrine sets out from the study of God, the infinitely perfect Being, *whose existence is here presupposed*, and continues in a long series of magnificent synthetic conceptions, — a chain of gold, as it were, of which the first links were forged by Plato, others by St. Augustine, and the last by Thomas himself. Here is the chain of reasoning in its logical sequence. God is Infinite. He alone possesses the plenitude of reality (XI). Every possible being (which will necessarily be outside of and distinct from Him) must possess its *ratio aeterna*, eternal reason, or explanation, in the Infinite Essence of God.[1] In other words, every finite being is a feeble and distant imitation of the Divine Infinity. There is no limit to the multitude of such possible beings. God, in knowing Himself, knows by means of the same intuitive vision all possible things, whether He calls them to existence, or not. Man, with his Intelligence, occupies a certain rank in this hierarchy of essences. In consequence, human nature or essence (that which each man is) stands in a certain fixed relation to the Infinite Being. Likewise, the human mind is a torch which has been lit by the Sun of Truth, i.e., the Divine Being, in order to reveal beings and reality, just as fire is made to burn. Thus, in the last analysis, God is the foundation of the reality and of the intelligibility of all that exists or is possible on the one hand, and of the aptitude of the human mind to attain to reality, i.e., to possess truth, on the other.

A conception like this results from a *coördination of many theories presupposed here and established elsewhere*, and forms a good example of the cohesion of scholastic philosophy as a whole (XIX, 2). The psychological aspect of the problem of truth is quite different. It rests upon the analysis of the facts of consciousness.

II. *The data of the epistemological problem.* The treatise *De Veritate* sets out quite clearly the data of the epistemological problem of certitude and truth.

(*a*) It reduces it to a reflective examination of those beliefs which we form spontaneously and which we find already in our minds, when we start our reflection.

[1] This is the theory of St. Augustine. The doctrine of the *rationes aeternae* or eternal reasons of things, is a modification of the Ideas of Plato, which begins to appear in the writings of the later Stoics.

(*b*) It regards truth as an attribute of the judgment, and not of the concept or of the simple apprehension.

(*c*) From the validity of judgments which are the results of reflection, it deduces that of spontaneous judgments which we formulate almost unconsciously.

Let us examine these points more closely.

(*a*) The epistemological inquiry consists of an examination of preëxisting beliefs by means of reflection. We are dogmatists from birth. As a result of the influence of education, our domestic and social surroundings, and also the spontaneous play of our faculties, we firmly assent to a great number of propositions which have entered into our minds without question or examination, like a crowd entering a free place of amusement. For instance, we believe that $2 + 2 = 4$; that our relatives exist; that there are things which we ought to do and others which we ought not to do, etc. Spontaneous and direct certitude precedes therefore the inquiry into certitude. Nay more: it is the former that is the object studied by the latter. Without spontaneous assertions, the epistemological inquiry would be void and empty. The critical or epistemological problem consists of scrutinizing these beliefs one by one, just as we separate the good grain from the chaff. We then examine the *motive* which leads us to eliminate some and keep others. "This investigation," writes Thomas, "consists in taking as the object of our inquiry, not only our subjective act of assent, but also the data to which we assent."[1]

(*b*) The process is an examination of the judgment, because truth is an attribute of judgment, and not of simple apprehension.

[1] *De Veritate*, q. 1, art. 9.

This is a doctrine which no Schoolman ever opposed. The idea of God, man, oak tree is neither true nor false, any more than the beings themselves which we call God, man, oak tree, are strictly speaking true or false. The reason for this is that truth consists in a relation of agreement or conformity, — *adequatio*. Now in that which is simple — such as an idea — there is no place for a relation.[1] The agreement or conformity of the content of an idea, such as good, living, derived from an acorn, with a being to which we refer it, exists only in, and by the judgment. Examples: 'God is good,' 'man is a living being,' 'the oak tree originates from an acorn.' Truth therefore in its strict sense belongs to the judgment,[2] and it is found in simple apprehension, or in the things themselves, only in a sense which is secondary, and rests upon the first.

(*c*) The examination by way of *reflection* enables us to test the value of those judgments which we form *spontaneously*, before and without the aid of reflection. There is no fundamental difference between the mental process in the case of primordial and direct assertions and that in the case of controlled or reflective assertions. But the only means we possess of examining the value of the former is to study them through the prism as it were of the latter. We shall find later that it is reflection which gives us the motive and criterion for retaining some of our spontaneous assents and rejecting others. It is also reflection which justifies our belief that judgments recognized as true attain to the external world in a way which is indeed inadequate, but yet relevant. We shall thus be enabled to draw the conclusion that the external reality is in the last analysis re-

[1] *Contra Gentiles*, I, cap. 59. [2] *De Veritate*, q. 1, art 3.

sponsible for our *spontaneous* assertions subsequently recognized as valid, and that accordingly, the human mind is capable of attaining to truth: its nature is to be in conformity with things. By *reflective* examination and reasoning, we recognize that our original mental operation is a valid and reliable one.

The two mental processes of which we have been speaking — the *reflective* examination of our assertions, and the *direct acquisition* of judgments to which we assent without any conscious motive for doing so — are clearly referred to by Aquinas, but he does not always keep the two quite distinct. He passes continually from the point of view of direct knowledge to that of reflection, and *vice versa*.[1]

[1] To my mind, this explains the differences amongst the interpreters of the texts of Aquinas concerning the notion of truth. Interminable discussions have been waged recently on this subject.

CHAPTER VI

MODERATE REALISM AND THE UNIVERSALS

I. *What the epistemological problem involves.* It has been indicated that the epistemological problem centers upon an inquiry concerning the validity of our spontaneous assertions. This inquiry resolves itself into *two* problems. First, the motive which leads the mind to establish a *relation* between a subject and a predicate in a judgment, and secondly, the validity of the respective *terms* themselves. Thus, when I say that a number *is* odd or even, or, that water boils at 100° C., I may inquire:

(*a*) What leads me to form a mental synthesis of number *and* odd or even; of water *and* boiling at 100° C.?

(*b*) What is the validity of these terms: number; odd; even; water; boiling? Are they mere mental products or do they refer to objects independently existent in an external world?

Aquinas does not formulate these two problems with modern precision, for he wrote at a time when idealism and scepticism were mere academic theses which no one took seriously; but his doctrine contains a solution of the two problems which we have indicated.

We will begin with the second, and his answer may be summed up as follows: "Our sense perceptions correspond to an external world, but their content is not adequate or complete. Again our abstract and general ideas (water, life, number, equality, etc.) correspond to a reality which is not solely a product of the mind, since it has been inferred from sense data."

II. *Objectivity of external sensations.* Generally speaking, according to the Schoolmen, the information presented to us by our senses is valuable, when working normally and when referring to their proper object, i.e., the special quality which each sense perceives to the exclusion of all the others (II, 2). In the case then of color, sound, odors, quantitative state and shape of bodies, the sense data of sight, hearing, smell, touch were considered as infallible. "The senses announce to us as they are themselves affected or modified." *Nuntiant uti afficiuntur.*[1]

Do our senses give us not only accurate information concerning the material worls, but also *adequate* knowledge? Scholasticism is prevented from admitting this in virtue of its basic principles, since in every act of cognition we contribute something of our own. Color cannot exist in my visual organ in the same way that it exists outside. But the problem of the extent to which our sensations correspond to the external world was neglected in the thirteenth century. The illusions of the senses were indeed known at that time; but as will be seen it was held that the erroneous information which resulted therefrom was not imputable to the

[1] *Summa Theol.*, I[a], q. 17, art. 2, or again: "Non decipitur (sensus) circa objectum proprium." The senses do not err concerning their proper object.

senses as such. At the most they conceded to the perceptions of touch the privilege of giving us the most intimate contact of all with reality, since continuous quantity, which is perceived by the sense of touch, is the fundamental attribute of material things, resulting from its very nature.[1] The Schoolmen were not aware of the distinction between primary and secondary qualities, in the sense introduced by Descartes and Locke. They held that quantity and extension do not constitute the essence of bodies (as Descartes thought), but rather its fundamental property.

III. *Real objectivity of abstract and general ideas. Universals.* An abstract idea has the same validity as a sensation, for it is from the content of sensation that the content of our ideas is derived. This content — including that of the highest and most general concepts, such as cause, life, substance — is contained in some way in the complexus of reality grasped by our senses; for, obviously, if they were not somehow in sense data, they could never have been derived from it.

But, there is a special difficulty when we come to consider what sort of correspondence can exist between reality and the concepts, each of which represent some

[1] Sensus tactus quasi fundamentum aliorum sensuum. *De Veritate*, q. 22, art. 5. It is possible to give a direct proof of the objectivity of external sensations by means of the principle of causality. A sensation is a non-necessary or a contingent event; it might not have taken place. In consequence, it has not within itself a sufficient explanation of its existence, — it depends upon something else (IV, 2). This 'other' is not-myself, for consciousness bears witness that I am passive in sensation. We accordingly conclude that this other is different from myself, and that there exists a real non-ego, which is the cause of the vital excitation culminating in the act of sensation. By elimination, it can be proved that this non-ego is none other than the material world. This reasoning, which we do not meet in the texts of Thomas, is quite in the spirit of his philosophy.

aspect of it. We came across the same difficulty previously, when dealing with the origin of ideas (III, 2). Here the difficulty concerns their validity. Outside us, everything is individual; the universe of the Schoolmen is a pluralistic universe, composed of single substances (VIII, 1), and everything which affects these individual substances is particularized. This being so, how can there be any correspondence between that which is concrete and singular (e.g., *this* living being, *this* material movement) on the one hand, and the abstract, universal notion (life, motion) on the other? Such is the famous problem of Universals, — or rather of the validity of our abstract and universal ideas.

Aquinas replies that the correspondence "between ideas and individual realities is not adequate, but is none the less faithful." To prove this, let us distinguish, as he does, between the *abstract* character of the idea, and its *universality*.

Consider the character of abstractness, which is the primordial one. We already know that the content of the concept 'man,' 'life,' 'local motion' is considered apart from those particular characteristics inseparable from each individual man, or each living being, or instance of local motion. As viewed by the mind, reality is neither *one* nor *multiple*; it seems to be completely indifferent to anything connected with number. The concept simply expresses the whatness of the reality 'man,' 'movement,' 'life.' In consequence, the abstract concept is a faithful representation of reality, for all the elements which go to make up the whatness or essence of 'man' or 'life' or 'motion' are found in each individual man or movement. Abstraction does not falsify (*abstrahentium non est mendacium*).

But the concept, although faithful to, is not entirely commensurate with concrete things, for the mind neglects the hall-mark of individuality which differentiates each particular man, living being or movement from others, and is incapable of knowing it. The abstract concept teaches us nothing concerning the essence of the individual. Moreover, not only is it true that the hall-mark of individuality escapes the mind, but our idea of a living being does not take account of the differences in essence between living beings of several kinds. The more abstract our knowledge is, the less it conveys of reality. The human mind has nothing to be proud of. Feeble and weak, but reliable in the little that they teach us, — such is the nature of our abstract ideas.

As for the process of universalization, which the abstract idea undergoes, this is entirely the work of the mind, for it consists in attributing to the content of the abstract idea an indefinite elasticity, and enables us to realize for instance that the essence of local motion or of humanity is found identically and completely in all instances of local motion, and in all human beings, whether actually existing or only possible. The characteristic of universality is the result of a reflection. Peter or John do not admit of multiplication. Universals do not exist outside of us; they exist only in our understanding. On the other hand, the whatness to which our mind gives the form of universality has a foundation in the extra-mental world. The process of universalizing neither takes away nor adds anything to the validity of the abstract ideas. *Universale est formaliter in intellectu, fundamentaliter in rebus.* Such is the condensed formula which sums up the thomistic solution of the problem. It was not discovered by Aquinas, but is rather the result of a slow and painful elaboration by Western thought in general. We find already in Abaelard, who flourished in the twelfth century, this doctrine of sound common sense, which fits in so well with the individualism of the Feudal system.

IV. *The Via Media between Naïve Realism and Idealism.* The thomistic doctrine of the correspondence between sense perceptions and abstract ideas on the one hand, and the external world on the other hand may be called the *via media* between naïve realism and idealism.

For the person whom we call a 'naïve realist,' reality is altogether independent of our knowledge of it, and our minds faithfully and accurately reflect things just as they are outside of us, in a merely passive way. The external world is reflected in consciousness as in a mirror. Scholasticism rejects this explanation of the absolute correspondence between the world of reality and the world of thought, as being too superficial, and instead gives us the conception of knowledge as a complex phenomenon, the product of two factors, — the object known and the subject knowing. The knower invests the thing known with *something* of himself.

Does this imply that the known object is simply a product of our mental organization, and that we know directly only our internal or subjective modifications? This doctrine, which is that of idealism, is equally opposed to the scholastic conception. For, according to the latter, the real object plays a part in knowledge, and is present to us in the act of knowing. We directly attain to reality and being, — so much so that the process by which reality acts upon us, the impression received, is discovered only as the result of reasoning (III, 1).

The epistemology of Aquinas is thus a moderate realism, a via media between exaggerated or naïve realism, and idealism. We attain to a reality itself independent of our act of knowing, and in doing so we become possessed of knowledge which is true, but inadequate. The process of psychological elaboration which goes on in the mind limits the field of knowledge, but does not disfigure it.

V. *The nature of the mental synthesis.* The second problem, which we must examine now, is to find out whether we have a plausible motive for joining two ideas in a judgment, and what is that motive. We may reply with Thomas: "The motive for the mental synthesis is the very *nature* of the represented objects." It is the nature of what we call water, ebullition; number, even, odd, which leads the mind to unite them, in the first case with, in the second case without the aid of experience.

This correspondence between represented objects constitutes truth. As soon as the connection between the content of the subject and that of the predicate appears to the mind, in other words becomes *evident* to it, the mind asserts it; and certainty is nothing but the firm adhesion of the mind to what it perceives.

It is important to note that the mind *merely perceives* the connection, without creating it, and herein lies the difference between thomistic and kantian intellectualism.

This doctrine applies to all judgments, and therefore to those directing principles which we have called the laws of universal intelligibility. For instance, in the principle of contradiction, the motive of our assertion is our insight into the incompatibility of being and non-being. The question of the applicability of these principles to existing beings follows immediately, once the existence of such extra-mental reality has been proved. Given that being exists, no matter of what kind, I have the right to declare it incompatible with non-being. Now if there is such a thing as contingent being, I am justified in applying to it that which belongs to the inmost nature of all contingent beings.[1]

Another corollary of this doctrine is that error is a property of judgment only. Error can belong neither to existing beings, nor to sensations, nor to simple apprehensions. Thomas employs this theory to solve the problem of sense illusions. The senses affirm nothing: they do not reflect upon the data, but present them just as they are, without any interpretation. That which is sweet to the palate of a healthy man appears bitter to an invalid.[2] Consequently the senses can neither correct themselves, nor find out the causes of their failures or illusions. Reason must intervene to test and control, and separate the true from the false. Error comes in with the judgment, for instance, when we rely on our sense-perception in predicating an attribute which the sensation in question is not competent to give (II, 2); or else a content which is disfigured because of the abnormal condition of the organism. In

[1] Certainly the principles of which we speak are independent of experience in the sense that the bond of union between the subject and predicate does not depend upon the existence of the material universe (III, 2), but *if this* world exists — and it does exist — then the principles of being must govern it.

[2] *Summa Theol.*, Iª, q. 17, art. 2. *De Veritate*, q. 1, art. 10.

any case, we possess means of controlling the illusions of the senses, and *an illusion which is capable of control is no longer really deceptive.*

VI. *Conclusion.* We perceive directly reality itself, and not our subjective modification of it. We perceive it thanks to a close collaboration between sense and intellect. The abstractive work of the mind, either superficial or profound, accompanies all our sense knowledge, and the mind has a tendency to unify all the data, and to arrive at an intelligible object that is increasingly complete. The mind is ever on the look-out for being, and seizes it whenever it presents itself. *Intellectus potest quodammodo omnia fieri.*—"The mind can in a way become all things." But it grasps reality imperfectly. The reflective study of the epistemological problem throws light upon the spontaneous operation of the mind.

Reflection makes it evident that truth is found only in a judgment. *Secundum hoc cognoscit veritatem intellectus quod supra se ipsum reflectitur.*—The mind knows truth inasmuch as it reflects back upon itself. It also makes it evident that mind in its spontaneous judgments seizes reality. Therefore Thomas is led to add that mind is made naturally to attain reality, *in cujus natura est ut rebus conformatur.*[1]

Taking what precedes into consideration, we may summarize thomistic doctrine in that well-known formula, current in the thirteenth century: truth is the correspondence between reality and the mind, *veritas est adaequatio rei et intellectus.*

[1] *De Veritate*, q. 1, art. 9.

CHAPTER VII

DESIRE AND FREEDOM

I. *Two forms of appetition.* Side by side with the life of knowledge, there is in us a certain vital tendency which leads us to seek for something other than ourselves, with the object of taking possession of it, and thereby procuring for ourselves some benefit. We wish to go for a walk, we long for a house of our own to live in, we seek to meet a friend. These examples show us that not only the external object, but also the exercise itself of our activities may become the subject matter of our desire. But whatever it may be that we desire, in every case we find that the motive which prompts our appetite is the benefit or the fulfillment which the object or activity in question will obtain for us. For man, like all other creatures, is only attracted by that which is good for him (VIII, 7) or, at least, that which in appearance is such.

In point of fact, our desires are directed towards a specific object only if it appears to be, that is, is known by us as suitable for us. *Nihil volitum nisi cognitum.* — "Nothing is desired unless it is first known." Appetition is the tendency or inclination of a knowing subject towards what it perceives as good. And just as knowledge is twofold in kind, so also the tendency which follows upon knowledge will differ, according as it succeeds an act of sense perception or an abstract representation. The former is given the name of sense appetite; the latter is referred to as the will.

II. *Sense appetite and the passions.* External and internal sensations may arouse our desires if they represent to us the attractions of external objects, or the charm or pleasure which accompanies the very exercise of our faculties. And since every sensation has a particularized, concrete content (II, 2) it will be *this* particular object of sense, or *this* individual sense activity which we wish to attain or accomplish when our appetite is set in motion.

The higher animals share with us certain sense movements which accompany our sense appetitions, such as love and hatred, courage, fear and anger. These emotions — or as the Schoolmen called them, these passions—are situated in the organism, and are by nature organic like the sensations and the sense appetitions. Thomas and the Schoolmen do not consider a passion as being of another kind than the sense appetition, which they accompany and intensify. If these passions or movements, which impel us towards a particular good or away from a particular evil present in sense perception, become violent and escape the control of reason, they disturb and may even dominate us completely.

III. *The will: its necessity and freedom.* In addition to these perceptions of some particular good offered by the senses, we possess a higher notion of that which is good: the idea of goodness as such. It needs little reflection to realize that the good can be thought of without limits, complete in itself, and universal. An irresistible impulse presses us towards the *good* as such, which we, human beings, alone among material creatures, are capable of conceiving. We are conscious of a deep, insatiable need of uniting ourselves to that which is capable of perfecting us in every way and forever. It is a need which is ever present, and acts upon us just as a weight attached to a lever continually exercises a downward pull. To this extent and in this sense *the will is necessitated or determined*, and is in a state of continual activity. This impulsion towards that which is suitable for us manifests itself in the initial attraction which we experience in the presence of any object which we look upon for the time being as good, without attending to its drawbacks. If the mind were to find itself in the presence of a real being which possessed the plenitude of goodness (and according to scholastic philosophy, God answers to this description) the will would see in it its object *par excellence*, that which is capable of satisfying all its needs, and it would cast itself towards God as iron towards a magnet.

But it so happens that in the field of our earthly activity we are confronted only by partially good things, and as soon as we reflect we become conscious of this limitation. It is thus in such a judgment following reflection that Thomism finds the explanation of liberty. Each good thing is good only from certain points of view, and is deficient from others. Consequently, the intellect presents us with two judgments. During the war, a soldier was often asked to volunteer for a task which must lead to certain death, and heroically, but freely, responded to the call. When he decided after a short reflection to die for his country, he was subject to the general attraction of that which is good (necessitated will), but he also found himself in the presence of two contradictory judgments: "to preserve one's life is good" (from one point of view), "not to preserve one's life is also good" (i.e., in certain cases, from another point of view). Thus we are called to *judge* and to choose between two contradictory judgments. Which shall I accept? It is the will which must make the choice, and the decision will be quite free, since neither judgment demands necessarily our assent. We choose freely the good as offered by one of both judgments, not because it is a *greater* good, but because it possesses *some* good.

It is true in a sense that we choose that which we consider to be the better. But to be quite accurate, we ought to add that there is a free intervention of the will in deciding what is better. In point of fact, the will can give its preference to either of the alternatives, by loading the scale as it were. When the moment comes for definitive choice, *deliberation* ceases and gives way to *decision*. By means of this analysis, Aquinas and Duns Scotus avoided the psychological determinism which appealed to other Schoolmen, — such as Godfrey of Fontaines, and John Buridan.

Liberty or freedom, of which we have just explained the psychological process, manifests itself in two forms: exercise of will, and choice. In the former, I decide to will, or to abstain from willing and choosing, and I differ my decision to some other time, — just as a citizen may decide to put a cross against the name of a candidate, or else may refuse to vote. This is known as liberty of exercise (*libertas exercitationis*). In the second case, I decide to will, and to choose one of two possible good things, like the elector who marks the ballot paper according to his preference, and this is liberty of specification (*libertas specificationis*). For instance, shall I go for a voyage or not? It rests with me to differ my decision or to decide at once. The Schoolmen also spoke of a third form of liberty: the moral value of the voluntary act. Of this we shall speak later on (XII, 3).

In every case it is easy to see that willing and liberty belong to the domain of consciousness, that external violence as such does not affect it, and that the carrying out of actions is a result of a free decision, but cannot constitute its essence. This does not mean that liberty is incapable of intensification or weakening by foreign elements.

IV. *Sentiments.* Before touching on the intensification or weakening of our free acts by other elements, it is well to note that affective states which precede our volitions, such as hope or despair, or which follow it, as pleasure or pain, etc., are regarded by the Schoolmen as modifications of the volitions themselves,— just as the passions are modifications of the sense-appetitions. They are simply certain modes of being of our desires in relation to an object. In consequence, pleasure and pain reside and have their seat in the desire itself, of which they are a sort of tonality. And just as any and every expenditure of conscious energy may become the object of desire, and be willed for the sake of the benefit derived from it, so in the same way the cause or source of pleasure is the conscious activity itself, when accompanied by certain conditions. Thus, in the apt expression of Aristotle, the pleasure of an activity (as for instance walking, or devoting oneself to something) forms a complement of the activity itself "as bloom in the case of youth." [1]

It follows from what we have said that Scholasticism knows nothing of a threefold division of our psychic activities such as that introduced by Tetens and Kant, who distinguished between knowledge, appetition, and sentiment. The last named is regarded instead as a natural dependent or the sense appetite of the will.

V. *Foreign influences and the will.* Since liberty presupposes a mind which reflects upon and judges its own judgment, it is itself a reaffirmation of the prestige enjoyed by the intelligence, undisputed monarch of our life as human beings. It is the mind which illumines our free choice, and clear mental vision is the primordial condition of the normal exercise of liberty.

But it is a matter of ordinary experience that our deliberations are affected by motives other than the real value of the objects under consideration. We are liable to be influenced by our emotions, passions, sentiments, and may be overcome by their disordered promptings, unless we take the precaution to discipline them by our reason. Or again, our spontaneous sympathy or preference for one of the alternatives may obscure the real value of the objects of choice. *Prout unusquisque affectus est, ita judicat.* As each one is inclined by his affection, so he judges. Anything which clarifies the mental vision of things increases thereby our liberty, and conversely, whatever darkens the intelligence dimin-

[1] ARISTOTLE, *Ethic. Nicom.*, L. X, cap. 4.

ishes our freedom. In the same way, threats, terrorism, external violence, or organic disturbances may suppress completely the exercise of reason and therefore leave no place for liberty in a particular case.

On the other hand, a man who is master of himself can enlist his passions, tendencies and pleasures in the service of a free decision and strengthen his liberty with all their psychological power. Such would be an explorer, or a missionary who found in his ardent temperament various elements which helped him to will more effectively and intensely a task freely chosen.

The interaction of the various activities of knowledge and of desire, and their dependence on the organism — which cannot be treated here in detail — lead us on to another doctrine, that of the unity of the ego. It is for didactic reasons that we have isolated our cognitive operations from our desires. In point of fact, the interdependence which we have already noticed between them shows that they are not juxtaposed like squares on a draught board, but might rather be said to compenetrate each other. We shall see later that all the human functions arise from one single source (X).

CHAPTER VIII

A UNIVERSE OF INDIVIDUALS

I. The Universe a collection of individual things.
II. Substance and Accidents.
III. Quantity, action, quality.
IV. Space and Time.
V. Relations.
VI. Grades of reality and multiplicity in each grade.
VII. Internal unity, truth, goodness.
VIII. Scholasticism the sworn enemy of Monism.

I. *The Universe a collection of individual things.* Let us imagine for one moment that by some great cosmic cataclysm the activity and movement of the universe were suddenly brought to a stop, and that we were in a position to dissect at our leisure the reality of which the universe is made up, in the same way that archaeologists excavate and study the interior of a house in Pompeii. What would a similar analysis of the world we live in reveal to the mind of a mediaeval schoolman? [1]

We should see in the first place that, in addition to the human race, there are thousands of other beings in existence, and that each one of these is a concrete individual thing, independent of and incommunicable to every other in its inmost nature, recalling the *πρώτη οὐσία* of Aristotle or the monad of Leibnitz. Individuals alone exist. We should find this individuality realized in each plant and animal in the domain of life, and, as

[1] We pass over the scholastic doctrine concerning the constitution of the heavenly bodies, for the sake of brevity.

for the inorganic world, in the particles of the four elements (air, water, fire, earth) or else in a compound resulting from their combination and itself possessing a specific state of being (*mixtum*). The chemistry of the Middle Ages was very rudimentary, and contained a mixture of truth and falsehood. On the other hand, the metaphysics, although closely bound up with this chemistry, is of an independent development. Indeed, it belongs to the particular sciences to determine what is the primordial particle of corporeal matter in each case. It matters little to the metaphysician whether this turns out to be the molecule or the atom (or even the ion or electron). Let us suppose that it is the atom: then the Schoolmen would say that the atoms of oxygen, chlorine, etc., are the real individuals of the inorganic world, it is to them that existence primarily belongs, and they alone possess internal unity.

What is the nature of these individual realities, which make up the universe?

II. *Substance and Accidents.* Let us examine more attentively any one of the many things which surround us on all sides, — a particular oak tree, for instance. This particular individual thing possesses many characteristics: it has a definite height, a trunk of cylindrical form and of a definite diameter, its bark is rugged, or 'gnarled' as the poets say, its foliage is of a somber color, it occupies a certain place in the forest, its leaves exercise a certain action upon the surrounding air, and itself is in turn influenced by things external to itself by means of the sap and the vitalizing elements which it contains. All these are so many attributes or determinations of being, or, to use the scholastic terminology, so many 'categories,' — quantity, quality, action, passion, time, space, relation.

But all the above categories or classes of reality presuppose a still more fundamental one. Can anyone conceive the being 'courageous' without someone who is courageous? Can one conceive quantity, thickness, growth, and the rest, without something — our oak tree in the above instance — to which they belong? Neither the action of growing, nor the extension which comes from quantity, can be conceived as independent of a subject. This fundamental subject Aristotle and the Schoolmen after him call the *substance*. The substance is reality which is able to exist in and by itself (*ens per se stans*); it is self-sufficient. It has no need of any other subject in which to inhere, but it is also the support of all the rest, which therefore are called *accidents*, — *id quod accidit alicui rei*, that which supervenes on something.[1]

Not only is it true that we *conceive* material realities in terms of substance and accidents, — and no philosophy denies the existence in our minds of these two concepts — but also that substance and accidents *exist* independently, and outside our minds. In the order of real existence, as in the order of our thought, substance and accidents are relative to each other. If we succeed in proving the external existence of an accident (the thickness of the trunk of the tree, for instance), we thereby demonstrate the existence of the substance (i.e., the tree). If the act of walking is not an illusion, but something real, the same must be equally true of

[1] "An accident need not be *accidental* in our use of the word, but it must be incidental to some being or substance." — WICKSTEED, PH.H. *The reactions between dogma and philosophy, illustrated from the works of S. Thomas Aquinas*. London, 1920, p. 421.

the substantial being who walks, and without whom there would be no act of walking.

Locke and many others have criticized the scholastic theory of substance. Their objections, however, rest on a twofold misconception of what that theory involves. First, it is supposed that one claims to know wherein one substance differs from another. Now scholastic philosophy never pretended to know wherein one substance differed from another in the external world. The concept of substance was arrived at not as the fruit of an intuition, but as the result of a reasoning process, which does not tell us *what* is specific in each substance, but only *that* substances are. We know that they must exist, but never what they are. Indeed, the idea of substance is essentially meager in content. We must repeat that we have no right to demand from a theory explanations which it does not profess to give.

A second misconception, that we can easily dispose of, represents the substance of a being as something simply underlying its other attributes. To suppose that we imagine something lying behind or underneath the accidents, as the door underlies the painted color, is simply to give a false interpretation of the scholastic theory, and of course there is no difficulty in exposing this conception to ridicule. But the interpretation is erroneous. Substance and accidents together constitute one and the same concrete existing thing. Indeed, it is the substance that confers individuality upon the particular determinations or accidents. It is the substance of the oak tree which constitutes the foundation and source of its individuality, and thus confers this individuality upon its qualities, its dimensions, and all the series of accidental determinations. This *tout ensemble* of substance and accidental determinations, taken all together, exists by virtue of one existence, that of the concrete oak tree as a whole. This doctrine will be developed in the next chapter, where we will consider the function of substance in the cycle of cosmic evolution.

No less than the substance of the individual man or oak tree, the series of determinations which affect it deserve our careful attention. Are the figure, roughness, strength, etc., distinct realities existing in one which is more fundamental, and if so in what sense?

To ask this question is tantamount to asking what are these determining or supervening states, which qualify a man or an oak tree as rough, strong, occupying space.[1] Let us review the chief classes of accidents, namely quantity, action, quality, space and time, relation.

III. *Quantity, action, quality.* The substantial subject which I call Peter, or any particular lion, does not occupy a mere mathematical point: its body is made up of parts in contact with each other (quantity) and which also exist outside each other (extension). The internal order which is the result of this juxtaposition constitutes the internal or private space or place of the body in question. Extension does not constitute the essence of a material thing (as Descartes taught), but it is its primary real attribute or property (*proprium*), naturally inseparable from it, and the one concerning which our senses give us the most exact information (VI, 2).

[1] It is clear from the above that substance is not quite the same as essence. Substance has its own essence, and accidents have theirs.

At the moment when we imagined a sudden petrification as it were of the universe, all these quantified subjects were engaged in *mutual action and reaction*. Chemical elements were in processes of combination or disassociation; external objects were giving rise to visual sensations in the eyes of animals and men. For, every substance is active — so much so that its activity forms a measure of its perfection (*agere sequitur esse*, activity follows upon existence) — and if a being were not endowed with activity, it would lack a sufficient reason for its existence. The action performed or undergone is a *real* modification of being, and cannot be denied unless we fly in the face of evidence. It is clear, for instance, that the thought of an Edison enriches the reality of the subject involved. Of course, we do not understand the *how*, or in what way a being A, independent of B, can nevertheless produce an effect in B. Once again we must not demand from a theory that which it does not pretend to give.

A *quality* of a being, according to the view of the Schoolmen, modifies it really in some specific character, and allows us to say of what kind it is (*qualis*). Rigorously speaking, this is not a definition, as the notion is too elementary to be strictly definable. The natural *figure* or shape, for instance a face or a mouth of a certain type, belongs to the group of qualities (*figura*). It arises from the disposition or arrangement of quantified parts, but it determines the being otherwise than in its mere extension.

Beside the figure of a being, the Schoolmen introduce a second group of qualities, consisting of the *intrinsic powers of action*, or capacities, — reservoirs, as it were, from which the action flows — for instance, when we say of a man that he is intelligent or strong-willed. They are known as powers (*potentiae*) in general, and as 'faculties' in the case of man. Thomas maintains that every limited being acts by means of principles of action. Only the Infinite Being acts directly through its substance, because in Him existing and acting are identical.

Finally, experience shows that faculties, by being exercised, acquire a certain real pliability or facility which predisposes them to act more easily or with more energy. The professional competency of an artisan, the muscular agility of a baseball player, the clear-headedness of a mathematician, the moral strength of a temperate or just man, — are all dispositions more or less permanent, lasting 'habits,' 'virtues,' which vary in different subjects, but all of which enrich the being of the one possessing them, since they collaborate with the power of action regarded as a whole.

IV. *Space and Time.* We can only touch on the question of space, which Aquinas, in common with other Schoolmen, considers at great length — not only the internal space proper to each body and which he identifies with its material enclosure, but space as a whole, the result of the juxtaposition of all existing bodies. This space is obviously a function of the material things which actually exist. The 'multitude' of such beings might be without limit, for there is no contradiction in supposing an indefinite multitude of material things each occupying an internal space finite in extent. Space as a whole, therefore, being the sum of these individual spaces, might be indefinite.

In the opinion of Thomas, time is really the same as the continuous movement or change in which all real beings are involved. But there is, by a mere mental activity, a breaking up, a numbering of this continuous movement into distinct parts, which in consequence necessarily appear to be successive. *Tempus est numerus motus secundum prius et posterius*[1] is the pregnant definition which Thomas borrows from Aristotle. Time is the measure of the (continuous) change, which the mind views as a succession of parts. The present and fleeting state of a changing being is alone real and existing. In the supposition of a motionless world which we made above, the present time would be a cross section of the universe, in its actual state, viewed in relation to the past and to the future. Now, since the multiplicity of beings is not necessarily limited, we may, by a process similar to our reasoning on space, conclude that time, the measure of changes which have *really* taken place or will take place in the future, may also be without limit in either direction.[2]

V. *Relations.* Passing over the passive, intransitive state (for instance, the state of being sad) which the Schoolmen regarded as a reality distinct from the subject which it affects, there remains the last of the categories, namely, *relation*. By means of this, the millions of beings which make up the universe, were, at the moment when we have supposed them to be arrested in their course, all bound up in a close network. By virtue of relations some things are *for* other things, or stand in a particular way *towards* other things (*ad alterum*).

[1] *De tempore,* cap. 2.

[2] Concrete space and time just discussed are altogether different from ideal space and time, which, by a process of abstraction and universalization, are separated from all relation to our universe and can be applied mentally to an indefinite number of possible worlds.

For instance, it is in virtue of a relation that several men are greater or smaller than others, stronger or weaker, more virtuous or vicious, jealous of others, well or badly governed, etc. Is the relation 'greater than' distinct from the size or quantity of the thing in question, the quantity being obviously the foundation of the relation? Thomas replies in the negative, and he would not have allowed that these relations have a separate reality of their own. My being greater or smaller than some particular African negro is not a new reality added to my figure or to my absolute size; otherwise, while retaining continuously the same figure, I should be constantly acquiring or losing realities, every time that African negroes increased or diminished their size, which is evidently ridiculous.

Let us continue the investigation of our dead universe. For there are two other static aspects of the *ensemble* of things: their hierarchical arrangement and multiplicity on the one hand, and certain attributes known as the 'transcendentals' on the other.

VI. *Grades of reality and multiplicity in each grade.* Although each material thing is itself, it is easy to see that there are many men all belonging to the same kind, in that these individuals possess a substantial perfection which is similar. On the other hand, being 'man' and being an 'oak' belong to different grades of reality.

The explanation is that every material substance has within itself a specific principle (we shall call it later substantial form), and the specific principle of the oak is altogether different from that of man, that of oxygen from that of hydrogen, and so on. The universe of the

Schoolmen is hierarchically arranged or graded, not merely by quantitative differences (mechanistic theory) but according to their internal perfection (dynamism). A consequence of this is that the substantial perfection of man or oak tree does not admit of degrees.[1] One is either a man or one is not: we cannot be things by halves. *Essentia (id est substantia) non suscipit plus vel minus.*—Essence or substance does not admit of more or less. The substance of man is the same in kind in all men. From this there will follow certain important social consequences which we shall take up later.

On the other hand, we see in one and the same substantial order of reality an indefinite number of distinct individuals. Whether we consider the past or the future, there are millions of oak trees, millions of men. Are individuals belonging to the same species just doubles or copies of each other? Have different men or different oak trees exactly the same value as realities? No. Although their substantial perfections are the same in nature and value, their accidents differ, and especially their qualities, quantity, and actions. Men or oak trees are born with different natural aptitudes, and their powers of action differ in intensity. Even two atoms of hydrogen (supposing the atom to be the chemical unit) occupy different places and have different surroundings, which is sufficient to differentiate them. *Equality of substance, and inequality of accidents* is the law which governs the distinction of individuals possessing the same grade of being so far as substantial perfections are concerned. We shall see that the exist-

[1] It is based ultimately upon an unchangeable relation with God, whose perfection it imitates.

ence of men together in society is simply an application of this principle.

VII. *Internal unity, truth, goodness.* Since every being, which really exists or is capable of existing, is itself an individual, it possesses internal unity. *Ens et unum convertuntur,* — being and unity are mutually convertible terms. Unity is simply an aspect of being. Parts of a thing, whether they are material or otherwise, all coalesce and do not exist for themselves, but for the individual whole. We must be careful here to avoid a wrong interpretation of this doctrine. The unity in question is the unity of the individual being, as found in nature; thus the unity of a man, an animal, a plant, or an atom. The unity of such an individual is quite distinct from that of a natural collection (e.g., a mountain, or a colony in biology), or an artificial one (such as a motor car, or a house). To these we attribute a nominal unity, for they are in themselves a collection of millions of individual things, united, in ways more or less intricate, by means of accidental states. A society of men is a unit of this kind.

Everything can become the object of intelligence, and in this sense, which we have met above (VI, 6), everything is *true.*

Again each being aims at some end by means of its activities, and that end is its own good or perfection. There would be no sufficient reason for a being to act, except for that which is suitable for itself (*bonum sibi*). Hence good is called "that which all things desire," *bonum est quod omnia appetunt.* Each thing is *good* in itself, and for itself. St. Augustine remarks that this is true even of such things as the scorpion, for its poison is harmful only to other beings. This tendency towards well-being, which is deeply rooted in everything, manifests itself in a way conformable to the specific nature of each being. It is blind and unconscious in the stone which falls, or in a molecule which is governed by its chemical affinities; it is conscious but necessitated or 'determined,' as moderns say, in a savage beast in presence of its prey; it may be conscious and in addition it may be free in the case of man.

Unity, truth, goodness, are called 'transcendental attributes,' because they are not special to some particular class or category of beings, but are above classes (*trans-cendunt*) and are found in all and every being.

VIII. *Scholasticism the sworn enemy of Monism.* The individuality of a number of beings involves their being distinct: one substance is not the other. Since the universe is a collection of individual things, scholasticism is the sworn enemy of monism, which regards all or several beings as coalescing into one only. For Aquinas, monism involves a contradiction. For, it must either *deny the real diversity* of the various manifestations or forms of the One Being, and in that case we must conclude that multiplicity is not real but an illusion; — or else it must *maintain that such diversity is real*, and then it follows that the idea of unification or identity is absurd.

In other words, the diversity and mutual irreducibility of individual substances are the only sufficient reason for the diversity manifested in the universe. We shall see later that the analysis of the data of consciousness furnishes a second argument against monism, so far as individual human beings are concerned (X, 1).

Although this reasoning can be applied to all forms of monism, Thomas Aquinas combats principally those systems which were current in his day, — the extreme Metaphysical Monism of Avicebron, the Materialistic Monism of David of Dinant, and the Modified Monism or Monopsychism of the Averroists of the West, which maintained that there is only one human soul for all mankind.

CHAPTER IX

THE PROCESS OF CHANGE

I. *Actuality and Potentiality.* Our supposition of a motionless and dead universe is after all only an artifice of our didactic method. For it is evident that the things which we have described are actors in a cosmic drama: they are borne on the stream of change, and nothing is motionless.

Molecules or atoms, monocellular beings or organisms, all are subject to the law of change. Substances, together with their accidents, are constantly becoming. The oak tree develops from an acorn, it becomes tall and massive, its vital activities are constantly subject to change, and the tree itself will eventually disappear. So also the lion is born, develops and grows, hunts its prey, propagates its kind, and finally dies. Again, human life, both in its embryonic and more developed forms, is a ceaseless process of adaptation. If we wish to understand the full meaning of reality, we must throw being into the melting pot of change. Thus the static point of view, or the world considered in the state of repose, must be supplemented by the dynamic point of view, or that of the world in the state of becoming. Here we come across a further scholastic notion, — namely, the celebrated theory of actuality and potentiality, which may well be said to form the keystone in the vaulting of metaphysics.

This theory results from an analysis of what change in general implies. What is change? It is a real passage from one state to another. Schoolmen reason thus: If one being passes from state A to state B, it must possess already in state A the germ of its future determination in state B. It has the capacity or potentiality of becoming B, before it actually is B. To deny this quasi-preëxistence, in fact, involves the denial of the reality of change, or evolution of things. For, what we call change would then simply be a series of instantaneous appearances and disappearances of realities, with no internal connection whatever between the members of the series, each possessing a duration infinitesimally small. The oak tree must be potentially in the acorn: if it were not there potentially, how could it ever issue from it? On the other hand, the oak is not potentially in a pebble rolled about by the sea, although the pebble might outwardly present a close resemblance to an acorn.

Act or actuality (*actus*) is any present degree of reality. Potency (*potentia*) is the aptitude or capacity of reaching that stage of reality. It is imperfection and non-being in a certain sense, but it is not mere nothing, for it is a non-being in a subject which already exists, and has within itself the germ of the future actualization.[1]

[1] We deliberately abstain from translating *potentia* by "power," as is sometimes done. "Power" has practically always an active sense which is

The duality of act and potency affects reality in its inmost depths, and extends to the composition of substance and accident, matter and form.

II. *The becoming of a substance.* To say that a concrete substance — for instance, this oak tree, this man — is in a process of becoming means that it is realizing or actualizing its potentialities. A child is already potentially the powerful athlete he will some day become. If he is destined to become a mathematician, then already in the cradle he possesses this aptitude or predisposition, whereas another infant is deprived of it. All increase in quantity, all new qualities, activities exercised and undergone, all the new relations in which the subject in question will be engaged with surrounding beings, all its various positions in time and space, were capable of coming to existence, before being in fact. Substance is related to its accidents like potentiality to actuality.

Viewed in the light of this theory, the doctrine of substance and accident loses its naïve appearance. A growing oak, a living man, a chemical unit, or any one of the millions of individual beings, is an individual substance which is in a process or state of becoming, inasmuch as its quantity, qualities, activities, and relations are actualizations of the potentialities of the

completely absent from *potentia* when contrasted with *actus*. An example will make our meaning clear. A sculptor is *in potentia* to the carving of a statue, but it is equally true that the block of marble is *in potentia* to becoming the statue. We should say that the sculptor had the "power" to make the statue, but we should hardly say that the block of marble had the "power" of becoming the statue. Hence the objection to the use of the word "power" here. A thing is in potency to that which will become, whether by its own activity, or the activity of something else.

substance. Leibnitz was in point of fact following this thomistic doctrine when he said: "the present is pregnant with the future."

But while Leibnitz taught also the eternity and the immutability of substances, which he called *monads*, Aquinas and the Schoolmen went further into the heart of things. It is not only the quantity or quality which changes when, for example, an oak tree grows, or its wood becomes tougher, it is not merely its place which changes when it is transplanted, or its activities which develop,— in all these cases it is the substance, the oak tree, which is so to speak the subject of these *accidental changes*. But the very substance of a body may be carried into the maelstrom, and nature makes us constant witnesses of the spectacle of *substantial transformation*. The oak tree dies, and from the gradual process of its decomposition there come into actual existence chemical bodies of various kinds. Or an electric current passes through water: and behold in the place of water we find hydrogen and oxygen.

III. *Prime Matter and Substantial Form.* When one substance changes into another, each has an entirely different specific nature. An oak never changes into another oak, nor one particle of water into another. But out of a dying oak tree, or a decomposed particle of water, are born new chemical bodies, with quite different activities, quantities, relations, and so on. Substances differ not only in degree, but in kind.

Let us look more closely into this phenomenon of basic change from one substance into another, or into several as in the case of water and the hydrogen and oxygen which succeed it. If Aquinas had been asked to interpret this phenomenon, he would have said that every substance that comes into being in this way consists ultimately of *two* constituent elements or substantial parts: on the one hand, there must be *something common* to the old state of being and the new — to water and hydrogen for instance — and on the other hand there must be a *specific principle proper to each.* Without a common element, found equally in the water and in the hydrogen and oxygen, the one could not be said to 'change' into the other, for there would be no transposition of any part of the water into the resulting elements, but rather an annihilation of the water, followed by a sudden apparition of hydrogen and oxygen. As for the specific principle, this must exist at each stage of the process as a peculiar and proper factor whereby the water as such differs from the hydrogen or oxygen as such.

This brings us to the theory of "primary matter" and "substantial form" which is often misunderstood. It is in reality nothing more than an application of the theory of actuality and potency to the problem of the transformation of bodies: before the change, hydrogen and oxygen were in the water *potentially.* The primary matter is the common, indeterminate element or substratum, capable of receiving in succession different determinations. The substantial form determines and specifies this potential element, and constitutes the particular thing in its individuality and specific kind of existence. It enables it to be itself and not something else. Each man, lion, oak tree, or chemical unit possesses its form, that is, its principle of specific and proper reality. And this principle or form of any one thing is not reducible to that which is proper to another. The form of an oak tree is altogether distinct from that of man, hydrogen, and so on.

IV. *Rôle of matter and form. Their relation.* Each thing that concerns the state of *indetermination* of a being follows from its prime matter. This applies especially to quantitative extension; for, to possess quantitative parts, scattered in space, is to be undetermined.

On the other hand, each thing that contributes to the *determination* of a being — its unity, its existence, its activities — is in close dependence upon the formal principle. Thus form unifies the scattered parts, it provides the substance with actual existence and is the basic root of all specific activity.

It follows from the above that matter and form cannot be found independently of one another in beings which are purely corporeal. They compenetrate each other like roundness and a round thing. To speak of a prime matter existing without a form, says Thomas, is to contradict oneself, for such a statement joins existence — which is determination — with the notion of prime matter — which is that of indetermination.[1]

We may now come back to the conception of individual substance from which we started (VIII, 1). A corporeal being consists of two substantial parts — matter and form — neither of which is complete. Only the being resulting from the union of both is a complete

[1] It is important to note that primary matter (*materia prima*) is altogether distinct from *matter* as understood by modern science. Matter as now understood signifies a substance of a particular kind (comprising 'matter' and 'substantial form' of the Schoolmen) together with extension in space, which is an 'accident.'

or individual substance, to which belongs the proper perfection of self-sufficiency and of being incommunicable to any other.

V. *Evolution or succession of forms.* The material universe presents us with an harmonious evolution. Reality mounts step by step from one specific nature to another, following a certain definite order. Nature changes water into hydrogen and oxygen, but it does not change a pebble into a lion; nor 'can one make a saw out of wool.' Things evolve according to certain affinities, and in a certain order, the investigation of which is the work of the particular sciences, and calls for patient observation. If there are any leaps in Nature, they are never capricious. Every material substance, at every stage and at every instant, contains already the germs of what it will be in the future. This is what is meant by the scholastic formula which states that "primary matter contains potentially, or in promise, the series of forms with which it will be invested in the course of its evolution." Prime matter is related to each substantial form, like potentiality to actuality. Hence, to ask, as some do, where the forms are before their appearance, and after their disappearance, is to reveal a misunderstanding of the scholastic system.

To sum up. Two kinds of change suffice to explain the material world. We have firstly the development of substances already constituted; thus an oak tree is undergoing development or change in its activities, its quantity, qualities, and relations, but it retains throughout the same substance: the change undergone is called accidental. In the second place, we have the change of one substance into another or into several, such as the change of an oak tree into a collection of chemical bodies: this change is called substantial.

Thus the evolution of the cosmos is explained as a combination of fixity and movement. Beings evolve, but everything is not new: something of the past remains in the present, and will in turn enter into the constitution of the future. The scholastic theory of the process of change is a modified one, a via media between the absolute evolution of Heraclitus and the theory of the fixity of essences which so much attracted Plato.

VI. *Principle of individuation.* The theory of matter and form also explains another scholastic doctrine, that of the principle of individuation. The problem to be solved is this: How is it possible that there should be so many distinct individualities possessing the same substantial perfection, or 'of the same kind,' as we say? Why are there millions upon millions of oak trees, and not only one, corresponding to one *forma querci*, one 'oak tree form'? Why should there be millions of human beings instead of one only? If everything was unique in this way, the universe would still manifest a scale of perfection, but there would be no two material things of one and the same kind. One thing would differ from another specifically, as the number 'three' differs from the number 'four.'

The 'monads' of Leibnitz present us with a conception of the world more or less on these lines. But the thomist solution is more profound. It is summed up in this thesis. *Extension — which pertains to prime matter — is the principle of individuation.*

My body has the limitation of extension, and in consequence there is room for your body, and for millions of others besides ours. An oak tree has a limited extension in space, and at the point where it ceases to occupy space there is room for others. In other words, without extension, or extended matter, there would be nothing which could render possible a multitude of individuals of the same kind. For, if we consider form alone, there is no reason why there should be a multiplication of a given form, or why one form should thus limit itself, instead of retaining and expressing within itself all the realization of which it is capable. *Forma irrecepta est illimitata.* — "A form which is not received in anything, i.e., an isolated form, is not limited or confined." But the case is different if the principle of determination is one which must take on an extended existence.

There is an important consequence which follows directly from this doctrine. *If there exist* some beings which are not corporeal, and whose principle of reality has nothing to do with extension and prime matter (pure forms; pure Intelligences, for instance), then no reduplication or multiplication is possible in that realm of being. Each individual will differ from one another as the oak-form differs from the beech-form or the hydrogen-form.

The last point explains why the problem of individuation is different from that of individuality. Each existing being is an individuality, and therefore a Pure Intelligence if such exists, also God, is an individuality. But individuation means a special restricted kind of individuality, i.e., a reduplication or multiplicity of identical forms in one group; hence the term specific groups, species.

VII. *Causality.* The theory of cause is a complement of the theory of actuality and potentiality, for it explains how the actualizing of a potency takes place in any given being. Causality is fourfold, because there are four ways of regarding the factors which account for the evolution of individual substances.

(*a*) The first and most apparent is efficient causality. It is the action by reason of which a being A which is capable of becoming A′ actually becomes A′. This action comes from without. No being which changes can give to itself, without some foreign influence, this complement of reality by virtue of which it passes from one state into another. *Quidquid movetur ab alio movetur*: whatever changes is changed by something other than itself. For if a thing could change its own state (whether substantial or accidental), unaided, it would possess before acquiring; it would already be what it is not yet, which is contradictory and impossible. Water is capable of changing into oxygen and hydrogen, but without the intervention of an electric current or something else it would never of itself take on these new determinations. A being which changes is of course a being which does not exist necessarily in this state of change. Hence the principle: whatever changes is changed by something other than itself, is an application of this more general principle: the existence of a non-necessary being demands an efficient cause (IV, 2).

However, this acting cause is itself subject to the process of becoming. The electrical energy could not manifest itself unless it is affected in its turn by the action of other efficient causes. The whole process resembles that which happens when a stone is thrown into still water: the waves spread out from the center, each producing the next in succession. Moreover, there is an additional complication, for every action of a being A upon another B is followed by a reaction of B upon A. Nature is an inextricable tissue of efficient causes, developments, passages from potency to actuality. Newton's Law of Gravitation, the Law of the Equilibrium of Forces, the Principle of the Conservation of Energy, are all so many formulas which set forth in precise terms the influence of one being upon another. Actions and reactions establish close connections between substances which are independent in their individuality.

(*b*) and (*c*). In addition to the efficient cause, scholasticism attributes a causal rôle to matter and to form, inasmuch as, in giving themselves to each other, these two constitute and explain the being which results from their combination. A particle of oxygen has for its constituent causes an undetermined element (primary matter), and a specifying element (substantial form), just as in turn the oak-substance or marble (secondary matter), together with the cylindrical shape or the human figure (accidental form), are constituent causes of a particular oak tree as a whole, or of a particular statue.

(*d*) Lastly, we have the final cause. The activities which flow from each individual being do not develop simply at random. Water is not indifferent to boiling at 90° C. or 100° C.: if it were so, we might expect to find all sorts of capricious jumps in nature. Since the same activities and transformations are continually recurring, we infer that there is in each being an inclination to follow a certain path, to obey certain laws. *Deus imprimit toti naturae principia propriorum actuum.* — God has impressed upon every nature the principles of its peculiar activities.[1] This inclination, which is rooted in the substantial form, and tends to produce the appropriate activities, constitutes the internal finality of each being. It is always present, even when an obstacle prevents its full exercise. *Natura non deficit in necessariis.*—Nature does not fail in necessary things.

In spite of disorders which appear at the surface of the physical world, and in spite of moral evil, both of which result from the contingent and imperfect character of the world, the internal finality proper to each being in the universe leads up to another finality, — which is external. The courses of the stars, the recurrence of seasons, the harmony of terrestrial phenomena, the march of civilization, are all indications of a cosmic order which is not the work of any single being — not even of man — but which proves to the mind of a Schoolman the existence of a Supreme Ruler of all, endowed with wisdom. Dante receives his inspiration from scholasticism, when he concludes the *Divine Comedy* by singing of the universal attraction of the world ever drawn towards its goal, which can only be God.[2]

This twofold doctrine of internal and external finality furnishes us with a strong teleological interpretation of the universe.

The hierarchical order that exists between the four causes results from their nature. Finality attracts

[1] *Summa Theol.*, Iª IIªᵉ, q. 93, art. 5.

[2] L'Amor che muove il sol e l'altre stelle.

(consciously or not) and persuades a being to exercise its activities. Efficient causality tends towards the end in view, and the result of action is a new union of matter and form. When an artist undertakes to chisel a statue, it is his purpose which directs the designs, the choice of the material, the chiseling itself. The first intention of the artist is the last thing to be realized. It is not otherwise with the aim of nature: in the order of intention the final cause comes first; but in the order of execution it is the last to be realized.

VIII. *Essence and existence.* We have not yet exhausted the analysis of reality. Each individual has been distinguished into substance and accident, and in every material substance we have found matter and form. In all these stages we have been studying essence, 'what the thing is.' Essence, however, has *existence*, and existence presents us with a quite new aspect of reality. Existence is the supreme determination of any being (*actus primus*). Without existence, the several essential elements which we have been considering would be merely possible; they would resemble the legendary horse of Roland, which possessed all perfections, but did not exist.

Moreover, these manifold essential elements (matter, form, accidents) do not exist in separation. They exist, says Aquinas, by virtue of *one* existence alone. It is the concrete oak tree which exists, the concrete lion, the actual man, Pasteur or Edison.

The theory of essence and existence completes the analysis of reality. We shall return to it in another chapter (XI, 2). We must first indicate the place of man in the world which we have been studying, and expound a body of doctrines sometimes known as the metaphysical side of scholastic psychology.[1]

[1] Scheme of metaphysical doctrines explained in Chapters VIII, IX, XI, 2.

- Essence (*essentia*)
  - Substance (*substantia*)
    - Prime matter (*materia prima*)
    - Substantial form (*forma substantialis*)
  - Accidents (*accidentia*)
    - Quantity
    - Action
    - Quality (shape, power, habits)
    - Time
    - Space
    - Relation
- Existence (*esse*)

The relation of act and potentiality is to be found: (*a*) between accident and substance, (*b*) between form and matter, (*c*) between existence and essence.

CHAPTER X

SOUL AND BODY

I. The substantial Ego.
II. Plurality of faculties.
III. Soul and body.
IV. Organic character of human operations.
V. Spirituality, Simplicity, Immortality.

I. *The substantial Ego.* The subject matter of scholastic psychology is not mere consciousness, or any single human function, but the whole man, the *ego* with the manifold activities of which he is the source. Even organic operations of nutrition and locomotion were dealt with in psychology. All these functions arise from one single source: the human ego. It is the same ego that eats, digests, moves, knows, wills, or suffers. This is so true that the intense exercise of one function can hinder the exercise of others. Thus, when I am digesting my dinner, I find the work of thought more difficult.

The ego is a substance, in other words a reality which is capable of existing by itself, in the sense that it does not exist *in something else* (VIII, 2). Moreover, the ego is an *individual* or *complete* substance. It is only the individual human being as a whole that exists. To such an individual we give the name of 'person,' in order to bring out the fact that in the human species the individual subject is endowed with reason. The definition of Boëthius still holds good: *persona est rationalis naturae individua substantia,* an individual substance of a rational nature. The true and unique human reality is therefore *this* particular human substance, *this* individual human being, which in the ordinary course of things is *this* person. To speak of 'collective personality,' or of a personality which would include other persons as parts, is to weave a concept from mutually contradictory notions. Indeed the members of such a collective personality could not themselves be persons, since a person must be independent of all other beings. Moreover consciousness naturally protests against the compenetration of my ego with another. We need not add that such a compenetration would mean the destruction of the freedom of the individual. Already we can see why scholastic moral and social philosophy emphasizes the value of individual personality, the psychological foundations of which are here laid down.

How does Thomas Aquinas prove the substantial and individual nature of the ego? He does so in arguing from consciousness, which testifies to its *existence* and to its *permanence*. Consciousness directly grasps my substantial ego in and through my activities. In thinking, in taking decisions, in walking, I attain to my own existing substance. However, it is important to note, that consciousness reveals only the *existence* of the ego, and teaches us nothing concerning its inmost *nature*. It tells us that the ego exists, not in what it consists. The best proof of this is the disagreement amongst thinkers concerning the nature of the ego, of the soul, or of man in general.

The permanence of the ego, as witnessed by memory, furnishes another demonstration that it is really and truly an individual substance. At the present moment I realize that I am the same person that I was five years ago, in spite of my many changes and activities since then. This permanence is an indication of the fact that I exist in myself, by my own right, so to speak.

II. *Plurality of faculties.* In order to harmonize the unity of the ego on the one hand, and the varied character of its functionings on the other, Scholasticism attributes such activities *as cannot be mutually identified*, such as nutrition, movement, sense knowledge, knowledge by abstraction, will, to immediate sources known as 'faculties' (VIII, 3). Thomas maintained that these faculties are really distinct from the ego. Doubtless, in the last analysis, it is the man who acts, but he acts by means of his faculties, which are deeply rooted in what may be called the substance of the man, but are at the same time distinct from it. Moreover, Thomas teaches that man's faculties of action are not only distinct from his substance, but that they are also really distinct from each other, e.g., intelligence from will. He bases this teaching upon the fact that they mutually influence each other, and that one and the same thing cannot be the subject and object of an action.

This already shows us that the whole doctrine is the result not of an intuition but of a reasoning process. The classification of the proximate principles of human action or faculties reduces itself to a catalogue of those activities of the ego which cannot be identified with each other. It is not a psychological, but a metaphysical explanation. Consciousness tells us nothing about the faculties or *energies* of the ego, apart from their exercise. Apart from thought, the mind remains a mystery to itself forever. "The human intellect has within itself the power of understanding, but *not of being understood except in so far as it is in a state of activity.*" [1] There are no means of getting at the mind-in-itself, nor of saying beforehand, as Fichte did, what objects it is capable of attaining. Nor does the theory of faculties tell us anything more concerning the precise nature of the action. For instance, to know that vision is a faculty adds nothing to our understanding of the activity of sight itself, but it sheds light upon the internal constitution of the acting subject; from the specific differences of human activities, it becomes evident that manifold principles of action must exist in one subject. Critics of this theory must bear in mind the elementary principle that we must not demand from the theory of faculties what it does not profess to give.

The same reasoning process which informs us of the existence of faculties also teaches us that the ego is composed of a soul and a body.

III. *Soul and body.* The substantial ego, or human individual, is not a simple being, but one composed of a body and a soul. This leads us to the current definition of man: a 'rational animal' (definition by logical parts) or 'a compound of body and soul' (definition by real parts). Like the other living substances — plant or animal, unicellular or higher organism — man is regarded as a compound made up of a body which plays the part of 'matter' and of a soul which acts as the 'substantial form.' If we recall what has been said in the previous chapter about matter and form, we shall understand the rôle of the soul and the body in man.

In the first place, since man really is a single whole, he is not a compound of two independent substances,

[1] *Summa Theol.*, I^a, q. 87, art. 1.

as Plato and Augustine held, but one substance. It is true that the extended body and the soul are *parts* of man, and parts of a *substantial* kind, since neither the soul nor the body exist in something else; but neither the soul nor the body alone is complete, or individual. Soul compenetrates body to the very essence of its being; they give themselves to each other, and thus form one unit.

This leads us to a second doctrine which is another application of the theory explained above. Since the human soul plays the rôle of substantial form, it confers on the whole individual man his specific character (IX, 4). It is on account of his soul, which is higher in the scale of perfection than the vital principles of animals and plants, that the functions of man include the specific human powers of knowledge and will. Similarly, the functions of animals are wider than those of plants because of the specific differences of their vital principle, as the vital principle of the lion differs from that of the rose tree. And in general all living creatures are different from and superior to inorganic bodies, such as a molecule of water or a loadstone, because they possess a form which is superior in perfection to any form found in the inorganic world. The human soul organizes its body from within and makes it its own body, by continually influencing and compenetrating it, and, when death puts an end to this union, the body ceases to be human and becomes something else.

It is because of this organizing rôle that Aquinas holds fast to the unity of the human soul, and this is a third doctrine which we want to emphasize. The question of the unity or plurality of the soul was a subject of heated discussions. If the individual is one being, it can only possess in itself *one organizing element* which confers this unity, although this one principle, if it occupies a high place in the scale of beings, like the human soul, possesses many kinds of activity which are found separately in inferior beings. The single human soul embraces the vegetative powers of nutrition and reproduction, the animal powers of sense perception and appetition, and in addition the powers of rationality. Here, as everywhere else, the psychological thesis of the unity of the soul is simply a particular application of the more general metaphysical doctrine of forms. There is a doctrinal solidarity throughout, and man takes his place in the vast harmony of the universe.

Finally — and this is a fourth application of the same general doctrine — the human body, which plays the rôle of matter, is the reason of the multiplicity of individual men within the human race. It is really the human body, as a product of generation, which is the principle of individuation; the precise reason why a man has such or such a soul, with its more or less perfect potentialities, is because he has such or such a body. The soul possesses the particular body for which it is fitted. It is true that the generation of a child is nothing but the becoming of a new substance, that its development comprises several stages specifically different in kind, and each more perfect than the one preceding, and that the immortal soul is created by God and united to the embryo only when the dispositions of the new organism are sufficiently perfect to require union with a *human* soul. But, although the spiritual and immortal soul is not a product of generation, nevertheless the parents in producing the body of their child assume the responsibility of fixing the potentialities of its whole being. The soul may be compared to wine, which varies in quantity according to the size of the cup.

IV. *Organic character of human operations.* Since the body is everywhere penetrated by the soul, since flesh, muscles and nerves derive from it their qualification of human, we can easily understand that not only our organic life, but also our psychic life, is closely bound up with the organism. Sensations and sense desires, which man possesses in common with other animals, have their seat in the organism, and are in consequence extended and divisible. In the case of abstract and universal concepts, scientific judgments and reasoning, the willing of good in general, and the free choice of particular goods, the soul is still held to the organism, since a disease of the nerves is sufficient to prevent the use of reason and to diminish or destroy our liberty. But there is an important difference to note here. The normal condition of the body is only an *external condition:* it is not responsible for the existence of thought or of will in their very essence. The body does not 'secrete' them. Thought and will are superior to everything that is material.

Why? Because the human concept has the royal prerogative of extending its dominion over reality, in depriving it, by abstraction, of all that makes it *merely corporeal,* multiple, and tied to time and space. It transcends the corporeal. The most profound notions, such as those of being, cause, force, substance, have a representational content so far detached from the corporeal or sensible that there is no contradiction in extending them to reality which is non-corporeal, or suprasensible, if such are proved to exist.

V. *Spirituality, Simplicity, Immortality.* We have seen that abstract knowledge has a content independent of material existence. In consequence, the soul too — of which abstract knowledge is an activity — shares the same character of independence. The vital principle of man — the soul — transcends matter: it is immaterial or spiritual. If it were otherwise, the effect (thought) would exceed the power of the cause, the less would produce the more and this would lead to the identity of contradictories. To be spiritual consists only in being able to act and exist without depending *intrinsically* on a corporeal co-element or body. It is true that our rational soul depends indirectly on the organism inasmuch as the soul draws from the sense perceptions material for abstract knowledge, and therefore the human soul naturally tends to be united to a body. But such a dependence does not affect the very essence or nature of the soul which is of a superior kind. Whereas the vital principles of plants or animals are *plunged* in matter (*immersa*) the human soul can subsist without body, although the body could not be without the soul.

Being spiritual, the soul has no quantitative or material parts in it. Moreover, self-consciousness does not admit of internal composition, since it is a process by which our soul imposes its whole self upon itself (*reditio completa*). If one folds a corporeal thing, for example a sheet of paper, only a part covers another part, but the whole sheet cannot be completely folded upon itself. Thus, if the soul were composed of quantitative parts consciousness would be partially but not totally imposed upon itself. Simplicity means absence of composition. It is a perfection of course, since in every composed being, the parts are limits of the whole, but we grasp it by way of negation, because, as has been seen above (III, 2), we have no proper knowledge of realities which go beyond the realm of sense perceptions.

Simplicity precludes the very conception of dissolution; the soul is not subject to death.[1] Only God could annihilate it. As the soul is naturally capable of surviving death, and as on the other hand it is naturally destined to inform or determine a body and to find in the senses the channels of its knowledge, a new union after death, with a body which will thereby become its own, does not involve any contradiction. Moreover, the intermediate state of the disembodied soul was regarded as provisional and incomplete.

In this way the chain of deductions unfolds itself, as did the great doctrines of Greek philosophy (spirituality, simplicity, immortality) which Aquinas regarded as truths accessible to human intelligence in virtue of its own powers. The arguments of Plato's *Phaedon* are completed by the reasoning of the *De Anima* of Aristotle, and the *De immortalitate* of Augustine. The Schoolmen without exception continue the line of Spiritualist philosophers. Materialism, which confuses sensation and thought, and which puts human individuality at the mercy of ever-changing chemical combinations, like a rose tree which withers or a lamb which is slaughtered, has an implacable enemy in Scholasticism.

[1] There are other proofs which are used in favor of immortality, such as the universal desire of survival, universal belief in life after death, etc.

On account of the spirituality of his soul, man occupies a central position in the universe. He is a spirit, but one destined to display its life in a body. He is midway between merely corporeal things and pure spirits. He is, to use a comparison dear to the Middle Ages, a *microcosm*, for all the perfections of reality as a whole meet in him in a wonderful alloy.

CHAPTER XI

GOD

I. Proofs of the existence of God.
II. God is Infinite Being or pure existence.
III. The Divine Attributes.
IV. Conclusion.

I. *Proofs of the existence of God.* It has been noticed above that the innumerable individual beings which make up the universe are subject to change, and that the change of anything whatsoever takes place by means of the action of some being other than itself. It is the action of B that causes A to become A . But the action of B itself implies a change in B, and this demands in turn the concurring causality of C, and so on (IX, 7). We cannot continue this process back to infinity. For in that case change would be without a sufficient explanation and therefore an illusion, whilst the existence and reality of change is one of the most evident things in nature. The setting in motion of a process of change demands a starting point, an initial impetus, whence the movement proceeds. This absolute beginning is possible only on the condition that a Being exists who is beyond all change, — in whom nothing can 'become,' and who is therefore immutable.

This being is God. Now, God cannot set in motion the series of changes constituted by actuality and potentiality except by an impulse which leaves free and undisturbed His own impassibility. For, if this initial impulse were to involve a modification, however slight, in the Primary Being, such modification would constitute a change, and require the intervention of a still higher Being. Thus the process would be endless unless God were the 'prime mover, himself unmoved.' [1]

Let us suppose that one decides to build a house, and that he wants it to have solid supports. To this end he must lay deep the foundations which are to support the building. He must continue to dig until he obtains a base of absolute fixity and security. But obviously he must finally call a halt in this work of excavation, if the building is to be commenced at all. We may therefore, nay must, conclude that the builder did in fact halt at some point in the earth, if *de facto* the building is there before our eyes.

The same applies to the scholastic argument which we are considering. Change exists as a fact, even as the house in question exists as a fact. Change stares us in the face: it is found everywhere in the universe. But if there were no starting point in the chain of efficient causation, the change itself could not exist. We are not in a position to deny the existence of the evolution of the universe: we must therefore account for it. To suppose an endless regressus in the causal series possible would be like imagining that one can suspend a weight from the end of a chain whose other end simply does not exist, since link is added to link to infinity.

Change is a certain indication of contingency or non-necessity, and this leads Thomas to a second proof of the existence of God, intimately related to the preceding: the existence of non-necessary beings demands the existence of a necessary Being. As soon as a non-

[1] *Summa Theol.*, Iª, q. 2, art. 3. Prima via.

necessary being is represented as existing, it ought to be referred to an influence external to itself, and here again a regression to infinity would not explain existing reality. One must stop at an absolutely necessary Being (*necessarium absolutum*), whose very essence it is to exist, and which finds its own necessity in itself. Such a Being is God.[1]

It is important to notice that the notion of contingency or non-necessity, upon which the argument rests, is independent of the notions of time and number. The principle of causality does not involve the concept of time. For, even if the series of contingent beings were without a beginning, these beings could not be made intelligible without the existence of a necessary Being.

It all comes, then, to this: if any given thing is real, the sum total of all those other things, without which the reality of that fact would be inexplicable, must be no less real. From the standpoint of metaphysics, God exists because the existence of the Universe demands Him. Hence the existence of God is not, as one might suppose, a further mystery requiring explanation in addition to the general mystery of the world. The scholastic argument for God's existence has exactly the same value as the principle of contradiction and of efficient causation.

Such are the principal proofs which Thomas Aquinas brings forward for the existence of God. There are others besides, all of which consist in an interpretation of facts. He sternly rejects the arguments known as 'ontological' which would better be described as 'logical,' such as those of St. Anselm and St. Augustine. From the content of our *idea* of God we cannot and may not

[1] *Ibid.* Tertia via.

infer the *actual* existence of God. The fact that existence is implied in the idea of an all-perfect Being is no guarantee of the real existence of such a Being. To pass thus from the conceptual order to the real order is tantamount to trying to suspend a picture from a painted nail.

II. *God is Infinite Being or pure existence.* Since material reality is alone proportioned to the knowing powers of man, since the mind only functions with the aid of the body (III, 2), God can only be known by us in an indirect way. "The highest knowledge which we can have of God in this life, is to know that He is above all that we can think concerning Him." [1]

In other words, we know God only by *analogy,* in attributing to Him all perfections — by *negation,* in excluding from these perfections all elements of imperfection — by *transcendence,* in removing every limitation which in other beings modifies a perfection. Our knowledge of God consists in knowing that He is infinite. Aristotle stopped at the notion of an unmoved mover. The Schoolmen added to it the notion of Infinity. Let us endeavor to show how this entirely negative concept does nevertheless attain to the Being who is the fullness of reality.

The Infinite Being, says Thomas Aquinas, having in Himself no potentiality, no limitation, is *pure existence.*[2] In order to realize exactly what this implies, let us avail ourselves of a simile, although in this subtle matter any comparison is necessarily inadequate.

[1] *De Veritate,* q. 2, art. 2.

[2] We must not confuse *real* Infinite, or God, which means pure perfection, with mathematical infinity, which deals with number and quantity.

"Imagine a series of vessels, with different capacities, which are to be filled with water; let there be tiny vessels, and vessels that will contain gallons, and great receptacles which are to serve as reservoirs. Clearly, the volume of water which may be stored in each vessel must be limited by the capacity of the vessel itself. Once a vessel is filled, not a drop can be added to its contents; were the very ocean itself to flow over it, the contents of the vessel would not increase.

"Now *existence* in a finite being may be likened to the water, in our simile; for *existence* too is limited by the capacity of every recipient being. This capacity is the sum total of the *potentialities* which from moment to moment become actual realities by being invested with existence. That oak of the forest which is invested with the most beautiful qualities of its species, and with the most perfect vital forces; that man of genius who is endowed with the most precious gifts of mind and body, — these possess the maximum of *existence* that can possibly be found in the species of oak and of man. But, be it remembered, the capacity for *existence* in each of these is limited and circumscribed by the very fact of the apportioned potentiality, or 'essence.' In this beautiful conception of Thomas, a vigorous oak has a larger measure of existence than a stunted one; a man of genius possesses *existence* in a larger sense than a man of inferior mind, — because the great man and the vigorous oak possess a larger measure of powers and activities, and because these powers and activities exist. But, once more, there is a limit even to their existence.

"On the other hand, to return to our simile, let us picture to ourselves an existence indefinitely uncircumscribed, say the ocean, without shore to confine or to limit it."[1] Such existence, with no qualifying or modifying adjective, is God. God is existence; he is nothing but the plenitude of existence. "He is the one who is," whose very essence is existence.[2] All other beings receive only some degree of existence, — the degree increasing in measure with increasing capacity. But they receive, in every case, their existence from God. Finite beings act upon each other, since, as we have seen above, the corporeal world is a network of efficient agents; they determine the capacity of the vessel, and the size varies unceasingly, but it is God alone who gives the existence according to the capacity in question.

III. *The Divine Attributes.* The study of the Divine attributes amounts to the inquiry by a close effort of reasoning as to what is implied by "Being which is existence without limit." Thomas enumerates these attributes, and establishes in turn God's simplicity, goodness, immutability, unity, justice, etc. He is never tired of stressing God's transcendent individuality, His knowledge and His government of the universe.

His transcendent individuality prevents Him from being confused with any of the limited beings to whom, by a free decree of His will, He has given or will give existence. Any confusion of God with finite beings would be incompatible with His Infinity, and therefore destroy God. A confusion of the *essence* or *existence* of the finite beings with the essence or existence of God

[1] *Civilization and Philosophy in the Middle Ages,* pp. 216–217.
[2] Ego sum qui sum. *Exodi,* III.

would lead us to a contradiction. For, a collection of finite essences, even if numerically indefinite, would nevertheless form a finite being. Nor could God's existence be the existence of all other existing beings, as Master Eckhart, a famous contemporary of Thomas, taught; for infinite existence is of another order than that of finite existence. *Per ipsam puritatem est esse distinctum ab omni esse.* — "On account of its purity, God's existence is distinct from all others." [1] Thus the Schoolmen not only reject the compenetration of finite beings in a single whole (VIII, 1 and X, 1) but also their compenetration with God. They deny monism in all forms. Creation *ex nihilo* by an act of free will is the only theory which can satisfy the exigencies of the metaphysics of reality as it actually is. In addition to the finite there must exist the Infinite, which can only be infinite on condition that it remains forever other than the finite, while at the same time the finite remains forever in dependence upon the infinite.

Since the principle of causality does not involve the notion of time, a creation for all eternity is not contradictory. On this subject, which was warmly debated in the thirteenth century, Thomas wrote: "It cannot be proved that man, or heaven or stones did not always exist." [2]

God's knowledge is perfect and identical with His essence. It must extend not merely to His own being, but to all other possible essences. God's knowledge and government of the universe is dealt with in the theory which has been called the 'system of laws.' [3] Thomas

[1] *De ente et essentia*, cap. vi.

[2] *Summa Theol.*, I^{a}, q. 46, art. 2. Mundum non semper fuisse sola fide tenetur, et demonstrative probari non potest.

[3] *Ibid.*, I^{a} II^{ae}, q. 90–97.

Aquinas there sets forth by way of synthesis the relations of subordination and dependence of contingent beings upon God. The eternal law (*lex aeterna*) is the plan of Providence such as it exists in the infinite knowledge of God. This plan is reflected in each and every being of the universe in a way conformable to its particular nature, and thus constitutes the 'natural law.' The effect of this *lex naturalis* is to lead each being to exercise its activities in such a way as to lead to its end, and so to contribute to the whole plan of Providence. It is blind and fatalistic in inferior beings, but in the case of man it is known by the reason, and it is in the power of human liberty to live in accordance with it or the contrary. *Lex naturalis nihil aliud est quam participatio legis aeternae in rationali creatura.*[1] — "The natural law (of mankind) is simply a reflection of the eternal law in a rational creature." We shall see shortly what a close relation there is between the natural human law and morality, and why it is that all positive laws ought to be based upon the natural law (XIII, 2, XV, 7).

IV. *Conclusion.* To Thomas Aquinas, the existence of God is not a truth which is immediately evident, but one requiring demonstration. We do not know Him in the manner in which we know, for example, the principle of contradiction or our own existence, but we have to view Him through the thick veil of the world of sense reality, which is between Him and us. Likewise, a reasoning process alone enables us to know some aspects, or attributes, of God's Infinity.

[1] *Ibid.*, I[a] II[ae], q. 91, art. 2.

Is such a knowledge of God anthropomorphic? Yes and no. Yes, in the sense that if we wish to say anything at all concerning God we must do so in a human way. No, inasmuch as we are fully aware of the inadequate and limited application of the 'names' which we give to the Godhead.

CHAPTER XII

PERSONAL CONDUCT AND MORAL VALUES

I. The Science of Morality.
II. The problem of ends or aims.
III. Voluntary acts and Free acts.
IV. Moral goodness of a human act.
V. Objective distinction between moral good and evil.
VI. Moral richness of an act.

I. *The Science of Morality.* The activity of man is characterized by teleology, i.e., he desires certain things as ends, and he wills other things as means to these ends. In this, he resembles all other natural beings, which are, as we have seen, endowed with this teleological character. But whereas these others tend towards their ends in virtue of certain internal inclinations themselves unconscious and not subject to control, man, being endowed with reason and liberty, is master of his own conduct, — "master of the acts which lead towards his end." [1] The study of human conduct as directed by us towards an end forms the subject matter of Ethics or Moral Philosophy. The knowledge which we thereby obtain is concerned with an order of things of which we ourselves are the authors, and not merely the spectators (XVIII, 2). For our conduct is our own work, and the resulting relations between us and the universe in general are what we ourselves make them.

[1] Dominus actuum ducens ad finem, *Summa Theol.*, I[a] II[ae], q. 1, art. 1, 2.

Starting from facts duly observed, Moral Philosophy discusses three general questions: the end in view, the act whereby we seek to attain it, and morality, or the relation of agreement or suitability between the one and the other.

II. *The problem of ends or aims.* It is a matter of common experience that our conduct is motivated by different aims: riches, honor, material pleasure, social positions, etc. All these are desired as being good things, for the only possible motive of action is our well-being, and the suitability of things or actions in view thereof. The good is that which all desire. Even a man who commits suicide, in order to put an end to some trouble or other, obeys the same law. Man's nature is to will *the* good, and all that is good. And when our knowledge puts us in presence of an external reality or an action "simply as desirable or suitable for us," we necessarily will it, unless indeed we first reflect, and as a result realize that "all is not gold that glitters."

The good which constitutes the end we aim at is always our own good. Nothing is more personal than conduct, and the ends we aim at in our lives. If the end be pleasure, fortune, or knowledge, it is still our own pleasure, our fortune, our knowledge. The end is a personal one, because man is an individual substance. Of course, the well-being of others enters as a motive of conduct, but it can only be a secondary one. It will be seen below that every human act is a *social* act, which benefits or harms a community. The realization of individual happiness is the sole reason for living in society. Hence it is still for our personal perfection that we care for the well-being of others. For instance, those who aid their neighbor see in their good work the accomplishment of an act which their reason approves, and which perfects them in their own eyes.

The Schoolmen are so convinced of the personal character of happiness that they raise the question whether an act of disinterested love is possible, even when God is the object. So that one could say in general: we love ourselves in the first place and others only secondarily.

Experience also teaches us that some ends are subordinated to others, and that all have not the same value. They are arranged in a hierarchical order: I go on a particular voyage, in order to do some business of a particular kind; this I want to do in order to make money; this again I want that I may be my own master, and so on. An end which is subordinated to another, or is useful, becomes a means. Now there must evidently be a supreme end or aim which dominates and underlies all the others. If not, I should never desire anything at all, and should never go beyond a mere platonic consideration of the possibilities of action. But we do make actual decisions, and in order to explain their actuality, there must be some real end towards which they are directed. Otherwise we should be led into an infinite regression, which is as absurd [1] in this connection as in the order of efficient causality (XI, 1). For, an infinite regress would render any actual decision impossible; and yet, particular decisions or acts of will are facts. What is this supreme end? We may say in the first place that it is my whole good or my good in general. But such a statement would be incomplete, for one would go on to ask where this whole good or good in general is

[1] *Ibid.*, I^{a} II^{ae}, q. 1, art. 4.

to be found. Here we are confronted with the theory of values. Concrete good things of many kinds lie within our grasp: pleasures of the body and of the mind, good health, fortune, friendship, and so on. All these correspond in a certain measure to our aspirations, but it becomes necessary to draw up a scale of their respective values, and this can only be done by the reason. Now our reason tells us that the *truly* human good ought to consist in that which will satisfy our specifically human aspirations, or, in other words, correspond to those faculties which are the highest we possess, and which make us human, namely intelligence and will. Things other than the intellectual will be good only as supplementary, so to speak, and as controlled by reason.[1]

The happiness which corresponds to our mode of being will consist in *knowing* and *loving*. To know in a perfect way, to penetrate all the mysteries of the material universe and to dominate it, and to know in addition by means of His works the great Creator of them all, God Himself; then to love in the same perfect way, to delight in knowledge for its own sake, and to cast ourselves towards God our Creator, — this will constitute philosophic happiness.

Doubtless, the man who desires good as such, perfect good, does not at once perceive that it is God alone who can fully satisfy the aspirations of his mind and heart. His reason arrives at this conclusion by the gradual elimination of objects other than God (XI,

[1] The supreme good of man is therefore something which is suitable, *bonum honestum*, i.e., something which harmonizes with a rational nature. It cannot be something merely useful, *bonum utile*, since this is by definition subordinated to something else. Nor can it be that which is merely pleasant, for pleasure is after all a corollary following upon activity (VII, 4).

1, 4). Until this process of reasoning is performed, man seeks for happiness, unaware that God is his happiness. "To perceive that someone approaches is not to know Peter, although Peter is the man who approaches. Likewise, to know that a supreme good exists is not to recognize God in it, although God is that supreme good." [1]

Doubtless, in this purely natural state of existence, we should have surmised that a knowledge and a love of another and higher kind, and out of the reach of our powers, was in itself possible, — we refer to a direct intuition of the Divinity, and a corresponding love. But in any case, we should have realized that it was beyond us, and we should have known also the reason why.

At this point Catholic theology intervenes, and states that this higher destiny and state, which surpasses the powers of our rational nature, is given us by grace.[2] God offers us supernatural happiness as a free gift. The "blessedness of abstraction" fades in "blessedness of vision," just as a shadow is absorbed in a ray of light.

The end of man, then, according to scholastic philosophy, is an intellectual one. To behold God, whether in His works, or face to face, is more essential for happiness than love itself, according to Thomas Aquinas, for love is after all a necessary consequence of such a vision. Surely no philosophy could give to knowledge a higher or more magnificent rôle than this.

It must not, however, be thought that the Schoolmen exclude other good things, such as physical well-being, from human happiness. Rather these things are con-

[1] *Ibid.*, I^a, q. 2, art. 1.

[2] *Ibid.*, I^a II^{ae}, q. 3, art. 8.

sidered to contribute to happiness as a whole, and since man has a body, his body ought to share in happiness just as his soul, always on condition that these complementary good things remain in due subordination to the human good *par excellence.*

In concluding this section, let us note that the supreme end of man, consisting in the full development of his powers of knowing and willing, is not beyond his grasp. Happiness is not a mirage. Scholastic Moral Philosophy is optimistic.

III. *Voluntary acts and Free acts.* Human conduct consists of voluntary acts, for it is the will that tends towards the good in general as presented to us by our reason, or towards any particular thing which exhibits the quality of goodness. 'Particular thing' must here be taken in a large sense, so as to include not merely external objects which we may wish for (as a landowner may wish to add a field to his property), but also any activity (eating, drinking, games, study) performed in obedience to the orders of the will. We have already seen that when confronted with a good thing which our minds regard as simply good and without defect, we necessarily will it (VII, 3). We cannot possibly destroy this tendency of our nature. Our will has an insatiable thirst for the good. Liberty enters only in the choice of things which are *partially* good, or which reflection shows to be limited in goodness.

It is therefore the voluntary act, and more especially the free act, which is endowed with morality. A morally good or bad act is above all a free act. Why is this?

IV. *Moral goodness of a human act.* A thing or act is *good* when it is suitable for us in some way. To live a life of pleasure, or to think only of getting rich, appears as good only to a sensual and grasping man. A thing or act is *morally good* only if it is *in agreement with the true end of man*, and contributes directly or indirectly to our real perfection (XII, 2). From the moral point of view, pleasure and wealth are neither good nor evil. They only become so when the will, guided by the reason, either does or does not employ them in the service of the truly human good, by allocating them their proper place in the scale of values. Goodness and moral goodness are accordingly not synonymous: the latter is only one species of the former. Morality will differ with the end assigned, since it consists in the relation between act and end. The conception of morality will accordingly be different in the hedonistic systems which regard pleasure as the only end, and in the intellectualist system of morality of the Schoolmen.

Morality belongs to the sum total of human volitions, but more especially to our free acts. Although the profound and necessary tendency of man towards the good in general is indeed endowed with morality, since it is that which sets the human will in motion, moral character belongs principally to the act which is freely willed; for once the fundamental tendency referred to translates itself into an actual volition, it will then be concerned with a concrete, limited good, which forms the subject matter of free choice. Thus man has the awful power of choosing his path. He can turn away from that which constitutes his true well-being, and attach himself instead to things which are doubtless endowed with real goodness of a sort, but are nevertheless destructive of his own true interests.

Liberty takes on a moral aspect when it is considered in conjunction with the end of human conduct. In consequence, anything which increases or diminishes liberty — dullness of mental vision, the duly ordered or disordered state of passions, bodily health or disease, education and habits — all will affect the *morality* of actions.

V. *Objective distinction between moral good and evil.* The end of man follows from his nature. The supreme human good is what it is because man has consciousness, is rational, and is endowed with free will. In the ultimate analysis, human nature, like all other essences, is founded upon an immutable relationship of similitude with God (V, 1). Since this is the case, the relation which exists between a human act and man's end must also follow from the *nature of things.* Whether we like it or not, it is what it is. Morality does not depend upon the caprice of men, and not even God Himself could change it. Whether we wish it or not, a prayer must draw us towards God, and blasphemy must separate us from Him. And, if life in society is an indispensable condition for the attainment of our individual ends (XV, 1), to help our fellows must be morally good, and to seek to destroy authority must be morally bad.

As for these acts which in themselves have no relation to man's end, and which are accordingly known as 'indifferent,' they will have a subordinate importance, and the end for which we freely perform them will give them a borrowed moral character as it were, which will make them really good or evil. The most banal of all our acts — such as going for a walk, or working in a laboratory — will possess its character of goodness or evil, because of the repercussion which it must ultimately have upon our lives or upon the lives of other members of human society.

VI. *Moral richness of an act.* From this it follows that the more an act conduces to the perfection of our nature, the richer will be its morality. Besides the intrinsic character of an act which makes it good or evil, and of which we have just spoken (*finis operis*), Thomas Aquinas calls attention to the *intention* (*finis operantis*), and the *circumstances* of this act, as being *two* other elements, which increase or diminish its moral goodness or evil. Thus, to open a subscription for the relief of the poor is a good act by its very nature, and no human intention could alter this intrinsic goodness (*finis operis*). But the vanity of him who organized the charity lessens the moral value of the undertaking. In the same way, this value increases, if he must undergo sacrifices or difficulties to attain his purpose. It may be noticed that these same elements (intrinsic character, intention, circumstances) affect not only the morality, but also the degree of reality of the act itself. Consequently they enrich or impoverish the personality from which all our activities originate.

CHAPTER XIII

OBLIGATION AND MORAL LAW

I. *Nature and extension of moral obligation.* The study of moral obligation is one of the chief features in which the Schoolmen advance beyond the Greek philosophers, who confined themselves to the study of the good. Among acts which are morally good some are obligatory; others are not. For instance, all men are not called upon to be heroes or martyrs, but it is required of all to respect the rights of others to life and property.

Psychologically, moral obligation manifests itself to us in the form of command, or compulsion, which pushes the will in a certain direction, and yet does not destroy liberty in those cases where there is room for freedom. For example, we are all aware that we should respect our parents, but we are all nevertheless free not to do so.

To what voluntary acts does this moral obligation belong? In the first place we are bound to will our end, i.e., our well-being, and to seek it where it is to be found —in that which answers to the deep-rooted tendencies of our rational nature — and not to look for it exclusively in those secondary goods which cease to be good when not controlled by reason. In the second place we are morally bound to will whatever is *indispensable* in order to reach this end, and to avoid that which must *of necessity* turn us away from it. Thus natural religion becomes a duty, since God is the end in which man finds his happiness, and since we are obliged to know God and to love Him, with the entire strength of our nature. With the Schoolmen, natural religion is a religion of love and inspires all human conduct. Therefore, God is not merely a frigid metaphysical skeleton, the changeless being which explains all change, but He enters into the whole moral life of man. Obligation in the case of the *necessary* means is a corollary from the obligation to seek the end. But obligation stops there. In order to get from Boston to New York, I *must somehow* cover the distance which separates the two cities, but I can get to New York by train or by steamer. So also I can freely choose between different means, when each of them leads to the end and no one is the exclusive way to reach it. This is the reason why all states of life are good, why neither marriage nor celibacy are obligatory, and why a man may choose any career which he thinks will enable him to reach his destiny. Hence moral obligation consists in the necessity of willing our supreme good, combined with the liberty of choosing the concrete objects wherein it is in fact realized.

What is the basis of moral obligation? The psychological fact of compulsion reveals moral obligation, but cannot be a sufficient reason for it, since we may ask further: upon what does this feeling rest? For the Schoolmen, moral obligation is founded upon human nature itself and its need of well-being. Such is at any rate the proximate basis of obligation. But the ultimate foundation is a Divine decree. God alone can dictate a law which binds morally; He alone can add the necessary sanction to it. Obligation and moral law stand to man in the same relation as the natural law to all beings: they concern the application of the eternal law to a nature which is rational and free.

II. *The Natural Law of Mankind.* Thomas Aquinas distinguishes between two kinds of commands dictated by the natural law to man. (1) First we have the fundamental command to act according to reason, "to do good and to avoid evil," and to follow some general precepts which flow from this fundamental obligation. For instance men are obliged "to preserve their own life and to ward off its obstacles . . . to know the truth about God and to live in Society."[1] These commands are the same for all men and for all time. They may become clouded over in certain cases, but they can never be altogether effaced, for they are a corollary of our inborn tendency towards our *real* well-being. It follows from this that human nature is radically sound, and that the worst of criminals is capable of moral reformation.

(2) In the second place we have principles which we may describe as circumstantial, since human conduct is necessarily bound up with conditions of space and time, and physical and social surroundings. Human reason must take the circumstances into consideration in enunciating a moral law. The more closely a law is applied to particular circumstances and cases, the more numerous will be the exceptions to the law, and these exceptions will be justifiable at the bar of reason. Accordingly, Thomas says that a moral law governs only the majority of cases, "*ut in pluribus.*" "Conse-

[1] *Summa Theol.*, Iª IIªᵉ, q. 94, art. 2.

quently, in contingent matters such as natural and human things, it is enough for a thing to be true in the greater number of cases, though at times, and less frequently, it may fail."[1] "From the principle that we must act according to reason, we can infer that we ought to return things entrusted to us, and this is true in the majority of cases. In certain instances, however, restitution would be dangerous and therefore unreasonable, as in the case where the one to whom the article was returned would make use of it to put an end to his life, or do harm to his country."[2]

III. *Fixity and variability of laws.* These conditions explain why in circumstantial laws — which after all are the only ones which regulate our daily life — we find both change and fixity. The historical and social circumstances may vary, and thus some elasticity in the moral laws becomes possible. But the fundamental precept, and the immediate corollaries from it, which are known by all and bind all, are fixed and invariable. They are as permanent as human nature and human reason themselves. They form a deposit in the depths of every human soul and an interior voice[3] informs us of them. They correspond to the unwritten dictates spoken of by Sophocles in Antigone, Cicero, the Stoics, and the Fathers of the Church, and which the Schoolmen incorporated into their comprehensive system of metaphysics.

[1] *Ibid.*, q. 96, art. 1. [2] *Ibid.*, q. 94, art. 4.

[3] The mind possesses a natural facility and permanent disposition to know the first moral precepts. It is called *synteresis,* which Thomas defines: *lex intellectus nostri inquantum est habitus continens praecepta legis naturalis quae sunt prima operum humanorum,* q. 94, art. 1.

CHAPTER XIV

CONSCIENCE AND MORAL VIRTUE

I. Conscience.
II. Responsibility and sanctions.
III. Moral Virtues. Prudence and Justice.

I. *Conscience.* The obligation to act in a particular way in a particular instance affects the will through the intermediary of an act of knowledge. This is evident from the data of psychology and ethics. I ought to know the moral law not only as expressed in more or less general principles by means of general judgments of the practical reason, but also as applying or not applying to the particular case before me. The act by which the reason applies a universal principle of morality to a particular case is the judgment of conscience.[1] The practical reason says: You must be honest in business and give to each his due. Conscience says: You must return to your customer the sum of a hundred dollars, above the price of the article sold to him, which he gave you by error.

A law which is not known cannot bind us, and we are never bound to act otherwise than our conscience tells us, even if its judgment happens to be erroneous. "We must say, unconditionally, that any act of will which goes astray from reason, whether that reason be correct or false, is evil."[2] In applying his principles in this way,

[1] *Summa Theol.*, I^{a} II^{ae}, q. 19, art. 5. *Conscientia nihil aliud est quam applicatio scientiae ad aliquem actum.*

[2] *Ibid.*, q. 19, art. 5.

Aquinas shows his breadth of view, and — let us remark incidentally — demonstrates the tolerance of the thinkers of the thirteenth century in religious matters. For if anyone thought in good faith that he would do wrong in becoming a Christian, he would do wrong in believing in Christ, although the Christian Faith is in itself good, and necessary for salvation.[1] For the same reason, a doubtful or 'probable' conscience does not bind or at any rate binds to a less degree. Obligation is a function of knowledge.

But we must add something further to this thomistic doctrine. It must not be supposed that *every* act of willing evil, under the impression that it is good, is morally upright, for man has a positive duty to instruct himself concerning his moral obligations, seek light on doubtful points, and weigh probabilities (XIII, 2). Error, doubt, hesitation become blameworthy if they are voluntary. Still, it remains true that anything which diminishes our clear vision of what we ought to do, such as prejudices, education, heredity, organic disease or weakness, fear, anger, and other passions, defects or evil tendencies in the will, emotions, etc. (VII, 5), reduces the moral character of an act, and likewise responsibility.

II. *Responsibility and sanctions.* Moral acts, whether obligatory or not, are imputable to the individual, in so far as they are freely performed. As Aristotle puts it, a man is the father of his acts as he is the father of his children.

Responsibility, relative to oneself or to others, involves merit and demerit. These are regarded by the

[1] *Ibid.*, q. 19, art. 5.

Schoolmen as the natural consequences of the use of liberty. If an act freely willed, moral or immoral, had *nothing to do* with merit or demerit, and if ultimately we could not fall back upon a system of sanctions (i.e., rewards and punishments) which need to be completed in a future life, — not only would the good cease to be rewarded and evil punished, but liberty itself would no longer have a sufficient reason. What would be the use of liberty, if its proper or improper employment were without effect upon our final happiness?

III. *Moral Virtues. Prudence and Justice.* The performing of acts morally good engenders moral virtue: it impresses upon the higher part of our being a lasting bent which inclines us to act well in all the circumstances of our life. Moral virtue is the result of moral conduct in the past, and the source of similar conduct in the future. The moral virtues are prudence, justice, fortitude, temperance (VIII, 3).

At the base of the moral life is prudence, the *recta ratio agibilium* — "right reasoning concerning things to be done" — which determines what act should be performed in particular circumstances. Certain primary and very simple judgments which are present in every mind (such as, for instance, "it is necessary to live in society") originate a tendency or inclination to act in accordance with them (for instance, a general tendency to do all that is necessary for life in society). Then comes a series of practical judgments which, considering all the circumstances (*consilium*, counsel), determine our choice. This in turn the will decides to follow (*imperium*). A prudent man is one who by the frequency of such judgments sees and decides rapidly and without hesitation what is to be done in a particular case. Prudence therefore belongs both to knowing and to acting, and exemplifies the intimate compenetration of knowledge and will in the unity of consciousness. Situated at the threshold of the moral life, prudence impregnates all the other virtues which guide us in our actions, especially justice, fortitude and temperance.

To understand the meaning of justice we must begin by considering the notion of right (*jus*). Right presupposes the living together of many human beings in a community. Since I have a personal end to attain, my acts are naturally means which serve for *my* own perfection. If they directly benefit others, then these others owe me compensation, and right, *jus*, consists precisely in this requirement of equity. "Right, or that which is just, is some work related to another according to some kind of equity." [1]

Justice, the virtue *par excellence* of life in society, is the psychological and moral state of a man who wills "firmly and permanently to render to each one his due." [2] It accordingly supposes a plurality of distinct persons, capable of bringing about this equity by means of their actions. "Since it belongs to justice to regulate human actions, this equity which is called for by justice must be between different persons, capable of action." [3] This is indeed called for by the individualism which runs through the Metaphysics and Moral Philosophy of Thomas. He never loses an opportunity of stressing the value of personality.

[1] *Jus sive justum est aliquod opus adaequatum alteri secundum aliquem modum. Ibid.*, q. 57, art. 1.

[2] *Perpetua et constans voluntas jus suum unicuique tribuendi. Ibid.*, q. 58, art. 1.

[3] *Ibid.*, art. 2.

Now, it is easy to see that the 'other than self,' for whose benefit justice exists, may signify an individual, or the community, and we thus obtain the division of justice into particular and social. For instance to give to a shopkeeper the price of an article purchased is to perform an act of private or particular justice.[1]

In the present chapter only particular justice is in question. Since right — that which is due to others — rests upon an objective equality, it is independent of our passions and affections. The same is true of the virtue of justice. On the other hand, fortitude, which regulates boldness and fear, temperance, which bridles our appetites, and other virtues, are directly related to our passions and our inner dispositions.

We can say that Thomas Aquinas retains for the group of moral virtues the Aristotelian notion "*in medio virtus*" on condition that the mean here is determined by reason, and differs in the case of different virtues. For instance, not to eat when one ought to, or to eat more than we ought, is not to observe the limits of temperance dictated by the reason. Where the virtues are concerned, we must keep close to reason.

The moral philosophy of Thomas Aquinas is in close dependence upon his Metaphysics. The moral value of personality, the end of man, the notion of moral goodness, the moral richness of a human act, are all established in a way conformable with the great principles of pluralism, of universal finality, and of the goodness of being.

[1] In this instance there is an exchange which brings about an equality, and it is called *commutative* justice. Besides, Aquinas considers as an act of particular justice the distribution to individuals of honors or distinctions which are at the disposal of the community, this being *distributive* justice. Commutative and distributive justice are the two divisions of private justice.

CHAPTER XV

GROUP LIFE AND THE STATE

I. The fundamental principle of group life.
II. The Unity of the group and the inalienable rights of its members.
III. The family.
IV. Origin of authority in the State.
V. Government is an officium or duty.
VI. The Sovereign People and its Representatives.
VII. The duties of the Sovereign, and the Legislative Power.
VIII. Social Justice and the Commonwealth.

I. *The fundamental principle of group life.* Man is intended by nature to form a society. The group life is necessary, for if left to himself in an isolated state, an individual would be deprived of the materials, the intellectual guidance, and moral support necessary for the attainment of happiness. The group life is necessary precisely and only because of this insufficiency of the individual for his own needs.

In this way, then, we justify the fundamental principle of life in society, which we may enunciate as follows: "The collectivity exists for the sake of the individual, and not the individual for the collectivity." Similarly, the well-being of a group will not differ in kind from that of the individuals which compose it.

The principle is a general one, and applies to domestic groups, political (village, city, state), religious (parish, abbey, diocese, Christendom), and economic ones (e.g., trade union or guild). It is based upon general ethics, which emphasizes the value of human personality, and this moral individualism, itself one of the most striking achievements of the civilization of the Middle Ages, is in turn linked to metaphysics, which recognizes no other existent, substantial reality than the individual, in the particular sphere in question.

II. *The Unity of the group and the inalienable rights of its members.* The collectivity therefore is not a substance as such, as is taught by some contemporary philosophers, and the very notion of 'a collective person' is contradictory (X, 1). Its unity is not the internal unity which belongs to a natural substance, and which ensures coherence within it, but rather an external unity. Each member of a group retains his value as a person, but his activities are united or rather coordinated with those of others. This is specially true of the State, "which comprises many persons, whose varied activities combine to produce its well-being." [1]

The unity of a social group or of the State is a "unity of functions" exercised by the different members. The only difference between natural groups (such as the family or the State) and artificial ones (such as a club or a political party) is that the working in common is necessary in the first case and not in the second.

Since the group exists for the sake of the members, it goes without saying that it cannot take away or modify those inalienable rights which are expressions of the personality, i.e., which belong to the individual as possessing a rational nature. Whether he be slave or free, rich or poor, ruler or ruled, an individual has "the right to preserve his life, to marry and to bring up children, to develop his intelligence, to be instructed, to hold to the truth, to live in Society." [2] These are

[1] *Summa Theol.*, I^a II^ae, q. 96, art. 1. [2] *Ibid.*, q. 94, art. 2.

some of the prerogatives of the individual which appear in the thirteenth-century Declaration of the Rights of Man.

Among the various natural groups, scholastic philosophers paid most attention to the family and the State.

III. *The family.* The family, which forms the cell of the social organism, comprises the husband, wife, children, and servants. The father is the head of this group, and derives his authority from God (XV, 4). Although the wife belongs in a sense to the husband (she is said to be some part of the husband), her independence relative to her husband is greater than that of children relative to their father, or servants to their masters. The subordination of a child to his father is complete, as is that of a serf to his master.

From this it follows that there will be stricter relations of 'justice' between husband and wife than between father and children, master and serfs, for, as we have seen above, justice requires a distinction (*ad alterum*) between persons. But always the individual rights of human beings remain. As for the serfs, the thirteenth century was not prepared to give them complete enfranchisement, but still their condition was altogether different from the slavery of antiquity and the early Middle Ages. Moreover, both canonical and civil legislation were constantly bettering their condition.

IV. *Origin of authority in the State.* Whether great or small, a State consists of a group of families under the authority or power of one or several persons. Whence comes this sovereignty, i.e., the power of a man to command and rule his fellows? Schoolmen reply that all power comes from God, and explain this as follows: The whole universe is regulated by the plan of Divine Providence, the eternal law of all reality (*lex aeterna*). Each individual thing contributes, by attaining to its own end, to the realization of this divine plan and the object of the whole. In consequence, man will play his part in the cosmic order ordained by God for the Universe precisely by achieving the destiny which belongs to him as a rational being and thus ensuring his happiness (XII, 1, 2). Now, since the group life was instituted in order to help individuals to attain their ends, the governing authority which forms a necessary element of a society (*ratio gubernationis*) must be a way of realizing the divine plan, and ultimately come from God also.

"Since the eternal law is the reason or explanation of government in the chief ruler, the reason for governing rulers must also be derived from the eternal law."[1] Rulers are therefore divine delegates. The theory is a general one, and applies to every kind of authority. In the case of the State, it does not matter by what means this divine power is transmitted, or in whom it is found. These are points for separate consideration.

V. *Government is an officium or duty.* The *raison d'être* of government determines its nature: it is utilitarian, an *officium*, 'office' or duty. The princes of the earth are instituted by God not in order that they may seek their own profit, but in order that they may ensure the common well-being. Even in the case of the papal theocracy, the idea of officium is always found with that of power, and the Pope describes himself as the

[1] *Summa Theol.*, Iª IIªᵉ, q. 93, art. 3.

servus servorum Dei, servant of the servants of God. Hence all treatises written for the use of princes and future monarchs condemn the capricious, selfish, arbitrary or tyrannical exercise of power.

Thomas builds up a whole system of guarantees in order to save the State from a government so completely opposed to its nature.[1] The guarantees are preventive in the first place: let the people carefully inquire concerning the candidate for power when choosing their ruler. Similar guarantees will exist throughout the monarch's reign, for his power will be controlled and countered by the intervention of other factors, as we shall shortly see. There are likewise repressive guarantees: resistance to unjust commands of a tyrant is not only permitted, but even enjoined. Thomas expressly condemns tyrannicide: one must go to any length in order to put up with an unjust ruler, but if the regime becomes quite unsupportable, then one must have recourse to that power of deposing the monarch which is the corollary of the right to choose one. This doctrine holds good whatever be the nature of government, — monarchy, aristocracy, or democracy. This brings us to the question of the depository of power.

VI. *The Sovereign People and its Representatives.* To understand properly the thomistic view on the seat of authority or of government in the State, we must distinguish as he does between two questions: (*a*) where is the seat of sovereignty in any case, (*b*) what is the most perfect form of government?

(*a*) At the outset, and in every state, sovereignty belongs to the collectivity, i.e., the sum total of individ-

[1] *De Regimine Principum*, lib. I, cap. 6.

uals. The people are the State. This is logical, for the only realities in society are the individuals, and apart from them the State is nothing, and moreover, government has as its object the well-being of all (2, 5). The doctrine of the sovereignty of the people is thus no modern invention.

But the collectivity or sum total of individuals is too complicated, too chaotic, to exercise power itself. In its turn, therefore, the collectivity delegates it usually, but not necessarily, to a monarch. For in theory one could choose instead an aristocratic or a republican form of government: "To ordain something for the common good belongs either to the whole community, or to someone taking the place of the community." [1] Thus power is transmitted by successive delegation from God to the people, and from the people to the ruler. The people hold it by a natural title which nothing can destroy, the king holds it by the will of the people, and this may change. There is, accordingly, at the base of the people's delegation to the king a contract, rudimentary or implicit in less perfect forms of society, explicit in States which have arrived at a high degree of organization. This will of the people, which can make itself known in many different ways, legitimatizes the exercise of power. Monarchy, in the opinion of Thomas, has the advantage of not scattering power and force. But he adds that circumstances must decide which is the best form of government at a particular moment in the political life of a nation. This gives his theory all the elasticity which could be desired.

(*b*) Still, he himself shows a very marked preference for a composite form, which he considers to be the most

[1] *Summa Theol.*, Iª Iªᵉ, q. 90, art. 3.

perfect realization of delegated authority. It is a mixed system of government, in which sovereignty belongs to the people, with the intervention of an elective monarchy, and an oligarchy which modifies the monarch's exercise of power. "The best regime will be realized in that city or state, in which one alone commands all the others by reason of his virtue, where some subordinate rulers command according to their merit, but where nevertheless power belongs to all, either because all are eligible as rulers, or simply because all are electors. Now this is the case in a government which consists of a happy combination of royalty, inasmuch as there is only one head, of aristocracy inasmuch as many collaborate in the work of government, according to their virtue, and of democracy or popular power inasmuch as the rulers may be chosen from among the people, and it belongs to the people to elect their rulers."[1] Aquinas affirms such political principles as universal suffrage, the right of the lowest of men to be raised to power, the appreciation of personal value and virtue, the domination of reason in those who govern or an 'enlightened government,' an elective system giving the means of choosing those most worthy, and the necessity of the political education of the people.

VII. *The duties of the Sovereign, and the Legislative Power.* In *De Regimine Principum*, of Thomas Aquinas, the ruler is charged with a threefold duty: he must establish the well-being of the whole, conserve it, and im-

[1] *Ibid.*, q. 97, art. 1. The *servi* are deprived of political rights because of their lack of adequate culture; heretics and Jews because Catholic civilization was then looked upon as the only existing civilization, and he who rebels against the Church necessarily rebels against the State also. But only political rights are here in question, not civil rights.

prove it.[1] First he must establish the common weal by preserving peace among the citizens (sometimes peace is referred to as *convenientia voluntatum*, — agreement of wills), by encouraging the citizens to lead a moral life, and providing a sufficient abundance of the material things which are necessary to it. The public weal once established, the next duty is to conserve it. This is accomplished by assuring the appointment of sufficient and capable agents of administration, by repressing disorder, by encouraging morality through a system of rewards and punishments, and by protecting the state against the attacks of external enemies. Finally the government is charged with a third mission, which is vague, more elastic: to rectify abuses, to make up for defects, to work for progress.

The means *par excellence* by which a Government is enabled to fulfil its threefold task is the power of making laws, i.e., of commanding. The thomistic theory of human or positive law, in its double form of *jus gentium*, law of the nations, common to all states, and *jus civile*, civil law, proper to individual states, is closely connected with the theory of law in general. For the civil law is, and can only be, a derivation from the natural law, and in consequence it ultimately comes from the eternal law (XIII, 2). Here once again the individual is protected against the State, for "in the measure that positive law is in disagreement with the natural law, it is no longer a law, but a corruption of law.[2] In this way the arbitrary element is banished from positive law, which is accordingly defined as "a rational injunction, made in view of the common good, and

[1] Lib. I, cap. 15.

[2] *Summa Theol.*, I^a II^{ae}, q. 95, art 2. Tribunals can correct the positive law by means of the natural law, if necessary.

promulgated by the one having charge of the community."[1] Positive law adapts to concrete circumstances the immediate prescriptions of the natural law, which in their abstract form belong to the law of nations. For instance, the law of nations enjoins that malefactors are to be punished. Positive law determines whether the punishment is to be by fine, imprisonment, etc. Positive law is therefore at once fixed and variable. It changes with circumstances, and it belongs to a government to modify it if necessary, always on condition that it bears in mind that every modification of a law lessens its force and majesty.

VIII. *Social Justice and the Commonwealth.* The common good is the result of good government and the reign of social justice. Thomas' views on social justice and solidarity are worthy of note. To understand them we must bear in mind what we have said of the notion of right and of justice (XIV, 3).

A compensation is due to each individual for whatever benefit accrues from his acts, and right is simply the requirement that this equal adjustment be made. To render to each one his due is to do justice. When the act benefits an entire community, social justice arises.

Hence, social justice demands two elements: (*a*) that the actions of the individual citizen or of the several members of a group be conducted in such a way that the community, i.e. all its members, shall be benefited thereby; (*b*) that, in return, the individual should receive from the community an adequate compensation.

Social justice thus understood rests upon a solemn affirmation of solidarity and mutual assistance. Every

[1] *Ibid.*, q. 90, art. 4.

human action, inasmuch as it is performed in a community, has its reaction upon that community, and benefits or harms it more or less, in some way.[1] The soldier who fights, the laborer who works, and the scholar who studies are engaged in social activities which, being such, do good to the whole community. Even the outbursts of individual passions admit of being referred to social justice, and "can be regulated with a view to the common good,"[2] since these outbursts intensify action, and every action has its echo in society.

Who ensures this convergence of individual activities? An individual citizen is obviously without the qualifications necessary for this task. It therefore belongs to the ruler to orient all good acts towards the common good of all. He is the *custos justi*, the *justum animatum*, — the guardian of right, the living embodiment of justice.[3] He is the architectonic chief (*architectonice*). Just as the master builder of the cathedral supervises the stonecutters, the carpenters, the sculptors, the painters, so that they may be ready at the proper time and place, so the master builder of social justice oversees all the diverse social activities and takes account of their relative importance in the community. It belongs to the ruler to see that the soldier fights, the scholar studies, the laborer works, etc., in such a way that all their activities may be directed to the realization of the harmony of the body politic. He must think out the best way of ensuring mutual assistance in order that everything may be of profit to all. His intervention will above all regulate all external actions: such as

[1] *Ibid.*, q. 58, art. 5. Cf. art. 6.
[2] *Ibid.*, art. 9, ad. 3.
[3] *Ibid.*, art. 1, ad 5.

diligence in work, temperance, meekness. But if necessary he will also occupy himself with actions which belong to the 'internal forum.' [1]

How is the ruler to carry out this high humanitarian mission? He can only do so by way of commandment. For, he possesses the virtue of justice as commanding (*per modum imperantis et dirigentis*), while the citizens share in it only as obeying (*per modum executionis*).[2] At first sight this looks like an intolerable and autocratic notion, a worship of the state, *étatisme,* which is bound to destroy individual autonomy. But these fears are groundless. The theory contains within itself the correctives for those abuses to which it seems to open the door, for the realization of the common good is the one and only motive which can render legitimate the intervention of the ruler. And this common good "*is no other than the good of each one of the members of the collectivity.*" [3] An arbitrary intervention on the part of the ruler which would be *destructive of individual good* — and thus of liberty — would be contrary to the common good, and as a consequence to social justice.

[1] *Ibid.*, art. 9.

[2] *Ibid.*, q. 58, art. 1, ad. 5.

[3] *Ibid.*, q. 58, art. 9. The ruler is not only the arbiter of social and legal justice, but he also contributes to the reign of particular justice: firstly, by distributing honors, distinctions, offices, etc., to the citizens in a way conformable to the requirements of distributive justice (*actus distributionis, qui est communium bonorum, pertinet solum ad praesidentem communibus bonis.* The act of distribution of common goods pertains only to the one presiding over common goods. I[a] II[ae], q. 61, art. 1); secondly, by enunciating in his courts of law the private rights (*jus*) of the citizens, as required by commutative justice (*determinare jus, judicium . . . importat . . . definitionem vel determinationem justi sive juris.* It belongs to a judge to define or determine that which is just or right. Q. 60, art. 1). Thomas condemns any intriguing in courts of law (*acceptio personarum*), and, in conformity with his moral optimism, he holds with the Roman lawyers that the accused should have the benefit of doubt (*ibid.*, q. 63).

The doctrine of social justice constitutes in the thomistic system an ideal which governments must never forget, and which they must realize to the fullest measure consonant with the actual conditions of a given civilization.

As to the compensation to the individual, which is owed by the community for services done, it is again the ruler who should decide as to the demands of social justice, although Thomas Aquinas does not insist upon this second aspect of the question.

CHAPTER XVI

THE CONSTRUCTION OF THE SCIENCES

I. Logic as a teaching method, and as a branch of philosophy.
II. Judgment.
III. Reasoning.
IV. Scientific systematization and its methods.

I. *Logic as a teaching method, and as a branch of philosophy.* Thomas asks whether logic is an art or a science, and comes to the conclusion that it is both.

The thirteenth century, in fact, considered logic as an art and retained the practice of exercises in logic. At the universities of Paris and Oxford, students were trained in the analysis of syllogisms, the refutation of sophisms, and the discussion of arguments for and against a given thesis. This kind of logic, which the early Middle Ages placed among the seven liberal arts under the name of *Dialectica*, is not strictly speaking a branch of philosophy.

But, side by side with this instrumental logic destined to discipline the mind, as athletic exercises train the muscles, the philosophers of the thirteenth century recognize and cultivate a philosophical logic which consists in a study of the architecture of human knowledge or of the methods adopted by the mind in the construction of the sciences, whether particular or philosophical. In this meaning of the term, logic itself is a science. It takes as its subject matter the whole content of knowledge, in order to study the laws which govern its coordination, synthesis, and systematization; and just as knowledge reaches an objective reality, logic too, in the final analysis leads us to truth and to certitude.

We may say that in the realm of their logic, the Schoolmen not only followed but also completed Aristotle.

II. *Judgment.* The most elementary construction of knowledge is the judgment, or the perception that a content of representation (for instance, 'white') applies or does not apply to another (for instance, 'snow'). It consists in the union or disunion of the two contents of representation (II, 4).

Science has to do with only one kind of judgment, the necessary and universal judgment, known as a 'law.' *Scientia non est de particularibus.* — Science has nothing to do with particular cases, or mere 'atomic propositions.' The logical law, or judgment, may be dependent upon, or independent of experience. Accordingly, it is included in one of the two classes of judgments which we have called above judgments of the existential and of the ideal order (IV, 2).

Let us consider each of these classes in more detail.

(*a*) With judgments of the ideal order, we are confronted with the process of pure deduction. An understanding and a comprehension of the subject and the predicate are sufficient in making the necessity of their connection evident, — just as in order to affirm the principle of contradiction it is enough to understand the meaning of being and non-being.

Mathematical judgments are of this sort; and the only difference between these and the directing principles of knowledge is that the latter are the foundation of *all* affirmation, whereas mathematical judgments relate only to a *special* field, namely quantity.

Moreover, the judgments of ideal order with which mathematics is concerned belongs to the same two types which we already discussed in connection with the directing principles. Thus mathematics comprehends:

(*a*) Judgments in which the subject considered in its essential elements includes the predicate, as for instance, $2 + 2 = 4$.

(β) Judgments in which the predicate is not included in the subject, although a comparison of the content of both is sufficient to make the necessity of their connection evident. That every number is either odd or even, remarks Thomas Aquinas, is a judgment belonging to that second type. The content of *odd or even* is not comprehended in the notion of *number*, but from the mere comparison of both it appears that being odd or even is a necessary property of every number.

(*b*) With the judgments of the existential order, we are confronted with the process of induction. A comprehension of the meaning of chlorine and oxygen is not sufficient to reveal the law governing their combination. Observation and experiences are needed in order to discover how they react to one another; and the law is obtained by applying to observation and experience such directing principles as those of sufficient reason and causality. For, these two principles justify us in concluding that the convergence and constancy of observed phenomena (as for instance the boiling of water under the action of heat) can only be explained by reference to a tendency on the part of the substance to act in a particular way, a tendency which is stable, and rests upon the nature of the thing in question (thus it is of the *nature* of water to boil at 100° C.). The Schoolmen did not study the methods of experiment with care and detail. This was only to be expected, seeing that the experimental sciences were in an undeveloped state in those times. But we already find among them — notably in John Duns Scotus, who flourished a few years after Thomas — a keen analysis of the methods of induction, or the ways by which we may pass from the observation of *particular* cases to the law which governs all.

III. *Reasoning.* A process of reasoning is itself a system of judgments, since it consists in passing from judgments already known to another less known or not known at all. The syllogism, which is the simplest expression of reasoning, consists of three judgments. It starts out from the enunciation of a law, or of a necessary relation, based upon the nature of things (for instance, "it is of the nature of a spiritual being to be simple, i.e., without parts"), and proceeds to show that this law applies to all or certain beings seen to be comprised under the extension of the law (for instance, "the human soul, belonging as it does to the category of spiritual beings, is endowed with simplicity"). The law, which is the foundation of the syllogism, belongs to either class of judgments, as it is dependent upon or independent of experience. The result of a syllogism is a new judgment, so that the judgment is the unit of logical construction, with which all knowledge begins and ends.

IV. *Scientific systematization and its methods.* 1. First principles of each science. — Isolated reasonings could not make a science. In their turn they are connected together like the links of a chain: each finds its justification in a previous inference. But there must be a beginning to the process, — there must be something from which the whole chain may hang. An infinite regression would render all knowledge impossible.

There are therefore at the base of *each and every* science certain indemonstrable judgments, known as the first principles of the science in question. They formulate certain very simple and evident relationships, and are derived from the subject matter of the science. Their enunciation may or may not presuppose observation, according to the nature of the subject matter of the science. Thus that $1 + 1 = 2$ is a principle of arithmetic; that the group life is for the sake of the individual members is a principle of social science. These principles, which do not admit of further definition or demonstration, constitute the limits and boundaries of each science. They consist generally of 'definitions,' inasmuch as they make clear what is the object studied by each particular science. We see, then, that besides the governing principles of *all* knowledge which are common to every science, like the principle of contradiction, each science has its *own* fundamental principles.[1]

[1] Scheme of scientific judgments. If we bear in mind that there are two types of judgments, namely judgments of the ideal and of the existential order (IV, 2), and that the first type includes two classes, we may establish the following scheme of judgments which are involved in any science.

A. Axioms, relating to all being, and common to all the sciences: these are judgments of the ideal order, especially of the second class.

B. Judgments proper to certain sciences.

1. Deductive sciences: judgments of the ideal order (both classes). They are either
   (*a*) the fundamental principles of the science in question; immediate and self-evident judgments. Example, $1 = 1$.
   (*b*) mediate, or calling for demonstration, e.g., the complicated theorems of geometry.
2. Experimental sciences: judgments of the existential order.
   (*a*) immediate or self-evident, e.g., "I think, therefore I exist."
   (*b*) mediate, e.g., "water boils at 100° C."

2. Material and formal object of each science.—The numerous reasonings which go to make up a science, together with its definitions and the first principles which constitute its basis, form one coherent whole, a unified system. The unity which runs through the whole, and is more or less evident according to the importance of each section, depends on the 'formal object' of the science. What does this mean?

The Schoolmen point out that in every science there is room to distinguish between the things themselves which are studied — the raw material of the science, its 'material object' — and the point of view, or aspect from which these materials are considered ('formal object'). For example, the human body is the material studied by physiology, but this only considers it from one point of view, namely, that of the functions exercised by its organs. This point of view is grasped as a result of abstraction, so that abstraction (II, 3) is the generative process which underlies all science.

Every reasoning or principle must express in some way the formal object of the science in question. Thus in physiology, every doctrine ought to be concerned with the functional rôle of organs. It is the 'formal object' which gives each science its distinctive character, and makes it what it is,—hence the designation of *formal*[1] object. Whence it follows, that two sciences may possess the same subject matter, may have the same 'raw material,' but unless they are to be identical, each must study this material from a distinct and separate point of view. Thus anatomy also studies the human body, but from the point of view of its structure.

[1] In *formal,* we find the determination, which belongs to the *forma*. Cf. p. 71.

If it were to concern itself with functions, it would trespass upon and identify itself with physiology, and one or the other would have to disappear.

Thomas applies this theory of the specification of sciences to philosophy and theology, which have to some extent the same material object, but of which the formal points of view are quite distinct. "A difference in the point of view from which the mind contemplates the object entails a diversity in the branches of knowledge (*diversa ratio cognoscibilis diversitatem scientiarum inducit*). The astronomer and the physicist both may prove the same conclusion,—that the earth, for instance, is round: the astronomer by means of mathematics (i.e., abstracting from matter), but the physicist by means of matter itself. Hence there is no reason why those things which may be learned from philosophical science, so far as they can be known by natural reason, may not also be taught us by another science so far as they fall within revelation. Hence theology included in Sacred Doctrine differs in kind from that theology which is part of philosophy." [1]

This justifies what we said at the beginning, that scholastic Philosophy is quite different from scholastic Theology, despite the relation between them, of which there will be made a brief mention toward the end of this work.

On these notions of the formal and material object, the scholastics rest their classification of the sciences whether particular or general, i.e., philosophical, and their division of philosophy (Chap. XVIII).

[1] *Summa Theol.*, I^a, q. 1, art. 1.

CHAPTER XVII

THE ESTHETIC ASPECT OF THE UNIVERSE

I. Art, Nature, and Beauty.
II. Objective and subjective aspect of beauty.

I. *Art, Nature, and Beauty.* Themselves contemporaries of a tremendous artistic development, which ranks the thirteenth century among the great creative epochs, the Schoolmen did not neglect the study of beauty in art. Any external product of man may possess beauty, — that of an artisan who makes furniture just as much as that of a painter of pictures or a builder of cathedrals. There is no essential distinction between arts and fine arts. If a man transforms preëxisting realities, then he is an artist, and the work of art is, says Dante, by reason of this act, a godlike creation.[1]

Nature also is beautiful. St. Bonaventure compares the universe to a magnificent symphony; Duns Scotus likens it to a superb tree. For the universe realizes and expresses order and purpose.

But beauty is not studied from the special point of view of nature or of art. Scholastic philosophy considers it in a general way, and esthetics becomes a department of metaphysics and psychology. Let us select therefrom some special points.

II. *Objective and subjective aspect of beauty.* Above all beauty is real and has an objective aspect: it is not a

[1] See author's *L'œuvre d'art et la beauté.* Conférences philosophiques, Louvain, 1920. Chaps. VIII and IX.

mere mental attitude. Beauty belongs to certain external things. Where is it found? In those things which realize and manifest an order variously described as the *commensuratio partium elegans* by Albert the Great, *aequalitas numerosa* by Bonaventura, *debita proportio* by Thomas Aquinas. Multiplicity of parts, variety, and unity of plan which combines the parts into one coherent whole, — such are the elements of order found in all beauty. The beauty of a being is the flowering of the reality which it ought to possess according to its nature, and which is called its natural perfection. Accordingly the unity which beauty expresses is a function of the specific principle to which each real being owes its fundamental determination, and which we have called its form (IX, 4). "The beautiful unifies everything it touches, and it is able to do so thanks to the form of the being, which it sets out in relief."[1] Perfection and form are both teleological functions. That is why the beauty of one thing is distinct from the beauty of another. An artist who wishes to paint the image of Christ "must reveal in the face the light of his Divinity."[2]

But not everything ordered is thereby beautiful. Order becomes esthetic only when *it speaks clearly and with no uncertain voice to a human intelligence* by means of sensations, and thus brings to the mind the pleasure of disinterested contemplation. Only the intelligence, which has being as its object, is able to penetrate through to the 'form,' and discern it in the midst of the sense impression and material data in which it manifests itself. Here once more scholasticism asserts its intellectualism.

[1] Albertus Magnus, *Opusc. de pulcro* (edit. Uccelli).
[2] *In Davidem*, Ps. 44, 2.

Thus the objective aspect of beauty is completed by the subjective aspect, or the impression which the beautiful produces within us. The order of things is necessarily adapted to an act of mental contemplation of which it is the content and terminus. Or, as the Schoolmen would say, order, and above all the form of the being, must shine forth to the mind. This relationship between the beautiful object and the knowing subject is seen in the theory of the *claritas pulcri*, or brilliancy of beauty. The more the form shines out, the greater and deeper will be the impression upon the human soul. It will be the 'substantial form' bursting through the perfection of a type or a species, as for instance when a Greek statue represents a typical human being; or more often some 'accidental form' may shine out,[1] as for instance an attitude of a mother smiling to her child. The brilliancy of the form is a principle of unity freely chosen by the artist in the work of art.

Beauty therefore does not belong exclusively to things as the Greeks thought, nor to the subject alone who reacts and enjoys, as some contemporary philosophers maintain. But it is as it were midway between object and subject, and consists in a correspondence between the two.

[1] ALBERTUS MAGNUS, *Opusc. de pulcro* (edit. Uccelli). Notio pulcri, in universali consistit in resplendentia formae (accidentalis) super partes materiae proportionatas, vel super diversas vires vel actiones.

CHAPTER XVIII

CLASSIFICATION OF THE SCIENCES AND DIVISIONS OF PHILOSOPHY

I. Particular and General Sciences.
II. Division of Philosophy.
III. Speculative Philosophy.
IV. Practical Philosophy.

I. *Particular and General Sciences.* At the time of the thirteenth century, the West possessed a comprehensive classification of the sciences, which we may well look upon as one of the characteristic achievements of the mediaeval mind, and which, in its main features, lasted up to the time of Wolf.

At the lowest stage we find the particular sciences,—which for the Schoolmen were the same as the experimental sciences. Such are Astronomy, Botany, Zoölogy, Human Physiology, Medicine, also Civil and Canon Law, which became separate and autonomous sciences in the twelfth century.

They derive their particularity (*a*) from the material object, which is particular. They are concerned only with a restricted section of the corporeal world. Botany, for instance, has nothing to do with economic wealth. (*b*) From their formal object, which, in consequence of what we have just said, cannot be grasped or abstracted from all reality, but only from a more or less restricted section of it.

But the detailed study of the sensible world by sections does not satisfy the mind. After the details, we seek for a comprehensive view of the whole, and this can only be furnished by philosophy. The man of science is like a stranger who explores a city bit by bit, and walks through its streets, avenues, parks, museums and buildings one after another. When at length he has wandered over the city in all directions, there still remains another way of becoming acquainted with it: from the top of a tower, the city would present to him another aspect, — its divisions, its general plan, and the relative disposition of its parts. The philosopher is just such a man: he views the world from above as it were, and tries to realize its general structure, for philosophy is a generalized knowledge of things, a synthetic view of that material world of which alone we have direct and proper knowledge, and then by extension, of all that is or can be (III, 2). It is human wisdom (*sapientia*), science *par excellence*. This general science or philosophy constitutes the second stage of knowledge.

In contrast to the particular sciences, philosophy derives its generality, (*a*) from its material object, — which is all that exists or can exist.

The man who takes in, by a single glance, the whole of a city from the top of his tower does not exclude any part from his regard, but he only looks for the general aspect of the whole, that which belongs to all and not merely to some of its parts. In the same way philosophy, instead of dealing with only one department of reality, takes in all the real.

(*b*) From its formal object which consists of points of view that affect and are found in all reality. Indeed these comprehensive views are possible only because the mind seizes in the immensity of reality certain aspects which are present everywhere and in everything, and which in consequence belong to the very essence of reality. Philosophy is defined as the investigation of all things by means of that which is fundamental in them and common to all. *Sapientia est scientia quae considerat primas et universales causas.*[1]

In other words, philosophy is a science which coordinates or makes a synthesis, for the materials it studies and the point of view from which it studies them are both characterized by generality. What are these general and comprehensive points of view or aspects which the human mind discovers in its study of the universe? This question brings us to the division of philosophy.

II. *Division of Philosophy.* Starting from a well-known classification of Aristotle, Thomas remarks that philosophical sciences admit of a first subdivision into theoretical and practical. The human mind (for all science, as we have seen, is a work of the mind) can come into contact with the real in general, or, as it was then called, the 'universal order,' in two ways. In the first place we may study this universal order such as it is in and for itself (θεωρεῖν, to consider), and look for its general features, without subordinating this knowledge to ourselves. This constitutes speculative or theoretic philosophy, the end of which is knowledge for its own sake. Or, in the second place one may study the universal order of things not as such, but in so far as it enters into relation with our conscious life (knowing, willing, producing). It is in this sense that this part of philosophy is called practical (πράττειν, to act).

Each of these two groups admits of further subdivision. Speculative philosophy comprises *Physics*

[1] *In Metaph.*, I, lect. 2.

(in the Aristotelian sense),[1] *Mathematics*, *Metaphysics*. Practical philosophy includes *Logic*, *Moral Philosophy*, *Esthetics*. Let us consider these various classifications in the light of the scholastic teaching concerning the construction of the sciences.

III. *Speculative Philosophy*. The division of speculative philosophy into Physics, Mathematics, Metaphysics does not correspond to three separate sections of being in the universe,[2] but results from the varying profundity of point of view or degree of abstraction with which we study the totality of things. Physics, mathematics, and metaphysics, all study the material universe as a whole, but each studies a particular aspect of all reality, change, quantity, and being, respectively.

(*a*) Physics. Everything is carried along on the stream of change, which the Schoolmen called *motus* (from *moveri*). The study of change in its inmost nature and in its implications is the first step in a general understanding of the universe. It is the task which belongs to Physics or to the philosophy of nature. Since man forms part of the world of sense reality, psychology is a department of physics, and the epistemological inquiry belongs to psychology.

(*b*) Mathematics. But there is in the sensible universe something more profound than change, — namely, quantity. For every change is closely bound up with conditions of time and space in which the change takes

[1] From φύσις, nature. Not to be confused with "Physics" in the modern sense, which is a particular science.

[2] As in the division introduced by Wolf, for whom speculative philosophy concerns itself with (*a*) nature other than man, i.e., Cosmology, (*b*) man, (Psychology), (*c*) God, i.e., Natural Theology or Theodicy. Wolf reserves the name Metaphysics for considerations common to all three groups.

place, while quantity, on the contrary, as studied in numbers and geometric figures, is grasped apart from the sensible condition of real quantified beings. Mathematics, which studies quantity and its implications, is for the Schoolmen a general and therefore a philosophical science,—a conception to which contemporary mathematicians tend to return.

(*c*) Metaphysics. Lastly, beyond change and quantity, metaphysics seizes in the things of experience the most profound aspects of reality, the strata which underlie all the others: being and the general determinations of being such as essence, existence, substance, unity, goodness, action, totality, causality, etc. These most general aspects of reality themselves constitute a synthetic view of the material universe. But while change, which implies duration in time, and while quantity, which is the primary attribute of bodies, depends on the material state of the universe, this state is not essential to the notion of being or those other ideas which are correlative to it. If there should be suprasensible beings, such as God, or the soul, then these metaphysical notions would be applicable to them, with certain necessary corrections. In this way natural theology and the non-experimental part of scholastic psychology really form part of metaphysics.

IV. *Practical Philosophy* is equally general in character, since through our conscious powers of knowing, willing, and producing we enter into relation with all reality. This general category includes logic, moral philosophy or ethics, and the philosophy of art or esthetics. Logic draws up a scheme of all that we know, and the method of constructing the sciences; as there is nothing that the human mind cannot know in some imperfect way, logic is a general science. Ethics, again, studies the realm of human conduct, and there is nothing in human life that cannot become the subject of morality. It is to be noted that politics and domestic ethics are, like individual ethics, merely applications of general moral philosophy. The philosophy of art deals with the order achieved by man externally through the guidance of reason, as when, for example, "he builds a house, or makes a piece of furniture." Philosophy of art here includes the study of the mechanical as well as the fine arts.

It is easy to realize that we have adopted this philosophical classification in the preceding chapters of this book.[1]

Particular sciences precede philosophy, and the latter must be in a sense based upon them. The programme

[1] As for mathematics, and the controversies of the thirteenth century concerning numbers, quantity, mathematical infinity, and so on, a clear understanding of these questions is not essential to our present aim, and we therefore pass over them in silence. It will be noticed that in the above classification the philosophy of art is placed in the group of practical sciences. We might, however, regard it instead as a third and separate group, corresponding to the poetical sciences of Aristotle.

The following is a schematic table of the scholastic classification of the sciences:

A. Particular or experimental sciences,

B. General or philosophical sciences:

1. Theoretical:
   - (*a*) Physics (in the ancient meaning of the term) of Philosophy of that which changes, including Psychology.
   - (*b*) Mathematics: philosophy of quantity.
   - (*c*) Metaphysics: philosophy of being.
2. Practical:
   - (*a*) Moral Philosophy, individual and social.
   - (*b*) Logic.
   - (*c*) Esthetics.

of the Faculty of Arts in the Universities of Paris and Oxford was inspired by this principle. The arrangement by which the particular sciences form the threshold of philosophy gives to the latter an experimental basis, or, as we should say today, a scientific foundation. General views presuppose particular or detailed ones to a certain extent.

CHAPTER XIX

DOCTRINAL CHARACTERISTICS OF SCHOLASTICISM

I. Moderation and the sense of limit.
II. Doctrinal Coherence.
III. Philosophy and Catholic Theology.

I. *Moderation and the sense of limit.* After this brief and elementary survey of the principal philosophical doctrines of Aquinas, we are in a position to discern certain characteristics of a systematic nature, which become evident everywhere. Two of these characteristics strike the student at once: moderation and the sense of limit; coherence and interdependence.

The sense of measure and of equilibrium appears throughout, because Scholasticism completes the naturalism of Aristotle with the aid of the idealism of Plato and St. Augustine. Thus it brings together what is best in Greek philosophy, tempers one element by another, and adapts the whole to the mentality of Western races.

The reader will easily recognize that this moderation was to be found in the first doctrine of which we treated, the theory of knowledge, which is a combination of spiritualism and sensationalism. The abstract idea is grasped in the sensation, and the one completes the other. The moderate realism of the Schoolmen is a via media between naïve realism and phenomenalism. Their theory of the union of soul and body places man in an intermediate position between the purely spiritual and the purely material. The limitation of actuality by potentiality and of form by matter gives us a moderate or mitigated dynamism; for the active or dynamic principle (form) expands into a passive and a quantitative element (matter), and thus we have a correction of the doctrine of pure energy. We find the same moderation in Ethics, in which intellectual happiness does not exclude the reasonable satisfaction of the body, and duty is harmonized with pleasure. The same appears in social philosophy where the individual good is harmonized with the well-being of the whole. In logic deductive and inductive methods assist each other and we could multiply similar examples. Its sense of measure makes scholasticism an eminently human philosophy.

One can say that a sense of proportion in all things is one of the characteristics of the neo-Latin and Anglo-Celtic civilization of the twelfth and thirteenth centuries, and that it is one of the finest heritages which these centuries have passed on to modern times.[1]

There is another reason for the great spread of thomism in the west, namely its doctrinal cohesion.

II. *Doctrinal Coherence.* Without doctrinal coherence, no philosophy could be vigorous or satisfy the human mind which seeks always for order and unity.

From this point of view, the difference which exists between the Schoolmen and certain modern philosophers is striking. Kant, for example, introduces in his philosophy compartments separated by tight walls. Science has nothing to do with moral conduct; private conduct and external legal relations are regulated by different principles. Or again, a man like Taine does not con-

[1] See *Civilization and Philosophy in the Middle Ages,* Chap. XIII, "Philosophy and National Temperament in the Thirteenth Century."

cern himself with the bearings of his theory of reality upon his moral duties. Similarly, a great many of our contemporaries split their lives into two parts — just as the Greek sceptics declared that certainty was impossible of attainment, in theory, and yet in practice acted as if they possessed certainty. Many men declare themselves unable to prove the existence of God, and nevertheless regard his existence as a postulate, necessary for action.

Nothing is more painful than these internal disruptions, which lead one to say that what is true and valuable in one context ceases to be so in another. And nothing is more opposed to the spirit of Thomism. Here we are face to face with a system or a doctrinal whole, in which everything is necessary for the rest. Truth, for Thomas, cannot contradict truth; and a doctrine, once established in one department, has validity in all others.

We have met in the course of this small book several instances of this coherence. Logic is closely bound to the psychological thesis of abstraction. Solutions of social problems rest upon the value of the personality. The theories of actuality and potentiality, of causality and of teleology, of essence and existence saturate the whole system. Everywhere we detect the metaphysics, which sustains all.[1]

Among the doctrines on which systematic coherence depends, there are three which are of fundamental importance. They resemble the pointed form which is found everywhere, in every corner and feature of a

[1] The reading of two or three articles of the two Summae of Thomas is sufficient to show that the subject therein treated is continually referred to and harmonized with other subjects, and given its proper place in the system as a whole.

Gothic cathedral. We refer to the intellectualism of the Schoolmen, to their emphasis of the value of human personality, and to the central place of God.

This intellectualism, of which Thomas Aquinas and Duns Scotus are the chief representatives, proclaims the supremacy of reason. To know is the noblest of the activities of a conscious being, — whether it be God, a limited spirit like an angel, or man. We apprehend reality by means of abstractions; and though such a mode of knowing is poor and restricted, nevertheless it is man's privilege, and raises him above the mere animal kingdom. If one looks back over the preceding chapters, he will find that the theory of abstract concepts extends throughout thomistic philosophy. If the abstract character of concepts were denied the process of judgment would become inexplicable; the possibility of science or general laws would be cut off; human liberty would become an illusion; moral ideals which rest upon the knowledge and love of God would vanish from life; even social life would change its character, for the entire system of Government is necessary only as a means to moral happiness.

The second fundamental doctrine is the value of personality. It declares each man to be an autonomous being, possessing his own body and his own soul, an agent with his own intelligence, will, and powers of action. Substantial or natural equality of men, the right to individual happiness, the protection of the person from the state, the mission of the state with reference to the individual, personal survival, — all are applications of the individualism which we wish to emphasize. Thomas has a profound aversion for anything resembling sacrifice of personal dignity and self-reliance.

Man is no exception to the general metaphysical rule that only individual substances exist or can exist; and God Himself, who created the world, is an Individual.

Finally, is it necessary to remark that God is found everywhere in the system? All the doctrines converge towards Him, as the radii of a circle converge towards the center. The God which Aquinas describes is not a *deus ex machina*, a pure product of reason, a metaphysical storehouse for Platonic Ideas. He is Infinite Life, and it is the divine life which gives a meaning to human life. For, God presents himself to man as the sole object worthy of his knowledge and love. An immutable and eternal relation exists between God and human nature (*lex aeterna*); and man, in recognizing the bonds which attach him to God, knows by this very act in what way he must direct his conduct to reach God. Family life, coöperation of the individuals in the social group, natural religion are means which aid the ascent of the human soul toward the Infinite. For the philosophers of the thirteenth century life is worth living, and all humanity moves forward toward happiness.

III. *Philosophy and Catholic Theology.* No one has emphasized the distinction between reason and faith to a greater extent than Thomas (XVI, 4). The one is not the other. But reason leads to faith, philosophy to theology. If Christian revelation is an historical fact— and no one doubted it in the West, at that time— philosophy reaches its culmination in theology. The life of the Christian appears as a more complete approach to God, the Being before whom all others are as if they were not. What Christian faith promises is a blessed vision, in which God reveals Himself to the soul, no longer in the pale images of the world of sense, but as He is.

Thus at once, the meaning of individual ethics and social philosophy changes. Life becomes a pilgrimage (*via*) toward our true fatherland (*patria*); duty done through the love of Christ takes on a higher value; the purely human ideal vanishes before the ideal of the *Beatitudes* and the *Sermon on the Mount;* social life is illuminated by the love of the other souls redeemed by Christ. Art itself becomes a symbol of the divine, and for Francis of Assisi, for Giotto, for the master builders of cathedrals, as well as for Dante, it appears as a way which leads the living generations toward heavenly immortality.

BIBLIOGRAPHY

GILSON, E.: Le Thomisme. Introduction au système de S. Thomas d'Aquin. Strasbourg, 1920.

GRABMANN, M.: Thomas von Aquin. Eine Einführung in seine Persönlichkeit und Gedankenwelt. München, 1912.

MERCIER, NYS, DEWULF. A Manual of Modern Scholastic Philosophy. London, 1917. 2 vols.

SERTILLANGES, A. D.: Thomas d'Aquin. (Collection Les Grands Philosophes.) Paris, 1910.

SERTILLANGES, A. D.: La philosophie morale de S. Thomas d'Aquin. (Collection historique des Grands Philosophes.) Paris, 1916.

SCHUTZ, L.: Thomas Lexicon. Paderborn, 1881.

Catalog of DOVER BOOKS

BOOKS EXPLAINING SCIENCE

(Note: The books listed under this category are general introductions, surveys, reviews, and non-technical expositions of science for the interested layman or scientist who wishes to brush up. Dover also publishes the largest list of inexpensive reprints of books on intermediate and higher mathematics, mathematical physics, engineering, chemistry, astronomy, etc., for the professional mathematician or scientist. For our complete Science Catalog, write Dept. catrr., Dover Publications, Inc., 180 Varick Street, New York 14, N. Y.)

CONCERNING THE NATURE OF THINGS, Sir William Bragg. Royal Institute Christmas Lectures by Nobel Laureate. Excellent plain-language introduction to gases, molecules, crystal structure, etc. explains "building blocks" of universe, basic properties of matter, with simplest, clearest examples, demonstrations. 32pp. of photos; 57 figures. 244pp. 5⅜ x 8.
T31 Paperbound **$1.35**

MATTER AND LIGHT, THE NEW PHYSICS, Louis de Broglie. Non-technical explanations by a Nobel Laureate of electro-magnetic theory, relativity, wave mechanics, quantum physics, philosophies of science, etc. Simple, yet accurate introduction to work of Planck, Bohr, Einstein, other modern physicists. Only 2 of 12 chapters require mathematics. 300pp. 5⅜ x 8.
T35 Paperbound **$1.60**

THE COMMON SENSE OF THE EXACT SCIENCES, W. K. Clifford. For 70 years, Clifford's work has been acclaimed as one of the clearest, yet most precise introductions to mathematical symbolism, measurement, surface boundaries, position, space, motion, mass and force, etc. Prefaces by Bertrand Russell and Karl Pearson. Introduction by James Newman. 130 figures. 249pp. 5⅜ x 8.
T61 Paperbound **$1.60**

THE NATURE OF LIGHT AND COLOUR IN THE OPEN AIR, M. Minnaert. What causes mirages? haloes? "multiple" suns and moons? Professor Minnaert explains these and hundreds of other fascinating natural optical phenomena in simple terms, tells how to observe them, suggests hundreds of experiments. 200 illus; 42 photos. xvi + 362pp.
T196 Paperbound **$1.95**

SPINNING TOPS AND GYROSCOPIC MOTION, John Perry. Classic elementary text on dynamics of rotation treats gyroscopes, tops, how quasi-rigidity is induced in paper disks, smoke rings, chains, etc, by rapid motion, precession, earth's motion, etc. Contains many easy-to-perform experiments. Appendix on practical uses of gyroscopes. 62 figures. 128pp.
T416 Paperbound **$1.00**

A CONCISE HISTORY OF MATHEMATICS, D. Struik. This lucid, easily followed history of mathematics from the Ancient Near East to modern times requires no mathematical background itself, yet introduces both mathematicians and laymen to basic concepts and discoveries and the men who made them. Contains a collection of 31 portraits of eminent mathematicians. Bibliography. xix + 299pp. 5⅜ x 8.
T255 Paperbound **$1.75**

THE RESTLESS UNIVERSE, Max Born. A remarkably clear, thorough exposition of gases, electrons, ions, waves and particles, electronic structure of the atom, nuclear physics, written for the layman by a Nobel Laureate. "Much more thorough and deep than most attempts . . . easy and delightful," CHEMICAL AND ENGINEERING NEWS. Includes 7 animated sequences showing motion of molecules, alpha particles, etc. 11 full-page plates of photographs. Total of nearly 600 illus. 315pp. 6⅛ x 9¼.
T412 Paperbound **$2.00**

WHAT IS SCIENCE?, N. Campbell. The role of experiment, the function of mathematics, the nature of scientific laws, the limitations of science, and many other provocative topics are explored without technicalities by an eminent scientist. "Still an excellent introduction to scientific philosophy," H. Margenau in PHYSICS TODAY. 192pp. 5⅜ x 8.
S43 Paperbound **$1.25**

FADS AND FALLACIES IN THE NAME OF SCIENCE, Martin Gardner. The standard account of the various cults, quack systems and delusions which have recently masqueraded as science: hollow earth theory, Atlantis, dianetics, Reich's orgone theory, flying saucers, Bridey Murphy, psionics, irridiagnosis, many other fascinating fallacies that deluded tens of thousands. "Should be read by everyone, scientist and non-scientist alike," R. T. Birge, Prof. Emeritus, Univ. of California; Former President, American Physical Society. Formerly titled, "In the Name of Science." Revised and enlarged edition. x + 365pp. 5⅜ x 8.
T394 Paperbound **$1.50**

THE STUDY OF THE HISTORY OF MATHEMATICS, THE STUDY OF THE HISTORY OF SCIENCE, G. Sarton. Two books bound as one. Both volumes are standard introductions to their fields by an eminent science historian. They discuss problems of historical research, teaching, pitfalls, other matters of interest to the historically oriented writer, teacher, or student. Both have extensive bibliographies. 10 illustrations. 188pp. 5⅜ x 8. T240 Paperbound **$1.25**

THE PRINCIPLES OF SCIENCE, W. S. Jevons. Unabridged reprinting of a milestone in the development of symbolic logic and other subjects concerning scientific methodology, probability, inferential validity, etc. Also describes Jevons' "logic machine," an early precursor of modern electronic calculators. Preface by E. Nagel. 839pp. 5⅜ x 8. S446 Paperbound **$2.98**

SCIENCE THEORY AND MAN, Erwin Schroedinger. Complete, unabridged reprinting of "Science and the Human Temperament" plus an additional essay "What is an Elementary Particle?" Nobel Laureate Schroedinger discusses many aspects of modern physics from novel points of view which provide unusual insights for both laymen and physicists. 192 pp. 5⅜ x 8.
T428 Paperbound **$1.35**

BRIDGES AND THEIR BUILDERS, D. B. Steinman & S. R. Watson. Information about ancient, medieval, modern bridges; how they were built; who built them; the structural principles employed; the materials they are built of; etc. Written by one of the world's leading authorities on bridge design and construction. New, revised, expanded edition. 23 photos; 26 line drawings, xvii + 401pp. 5⅜ x 8. T431 Paperbound **$1.95**

HISTORY OF MATHEMATICS, D. E. Smith. Most comprehensive non-technical history of math in English. In two volumes. Vol. I: A chronological examination of the growth of mathematics from primitive concepts up to 1900. Vol. II: The development of ideas in specific fields and areas, up through elementary calculus. The lives and works of over a thousand mathematicians are covered; thousands of specific historical problems and their solutions are clearly explained. Total of 510 illustrations, 1355pp. 5⅜ x 8. Set boxed in attractive container. T429, T430 Paperbound, the set **$5.00**

PHILOSOPHY AND THE PHYSICISTS, L. S. Stebbing. A philosopher examines the philosophical implications of modern science by posing a lively critical attack on the popular science expositions of Sir James Jeans and Arthur Eddington. xvi + 295pp. 5⅜ x 8.
T480 Paperbound **$1.65**

ON MATHEMATICS AND MATHEMATICIANS, R. E. Moritz. The first collection of quotations by and about mathematicians in English. 1140 anecdotes, aphorisms, definitions, speculations, etc. give both mathematicians and layman stimulating new insights into what mathematics is, and into the personalities of the great mathematicians from Archimedes to Euler, Gauss, Klein, Weierstrass. Invaluable to teachers, writers. Extensive cross index. 410pp. 5⅜ x 8.
T489 Paperbound **$1.95**

NATURAL SCIENCE, BIOLOGY, GEOLOGY, TRAVEL

A SHORT HISTORY OF ANATOMY AND PHYSIOLOGY FROM THE GREEKS TO HARVEY, C. Singer. A great medical historian's fascinating intermediate account of the slow advance of anatomical and physiological knowledge from pre-scientific times to Vesalius, Harvey. 139 unusually interesting illustrations. 221pp. 5⅜ x 8. T389 Paperbound **$1.75**

THE BEHAVIOUR AND SOCIAL LIFE OF HONEYBEES, Ronald Ribbands. The most comprehensive, lucid and authoritative book on bee habits, communication, duties, cell life, motivations, etc. "A MUST for every scientist, experimenter, and educator, and a happy and valuable selection for all interested in the honeybee," AMERICAN BEE JOURNAL. 690-item bibliography. 127 illus.; 11 photographic plates. 352pp. 5⅜ x 8⅜. S410 Clothbound **$4.50**

TRAVELS OF WILLIAM BARTRAM, edited by **Mark Van Doren.** One of the 18th century's most delightful books, and one of the few first-hand sources of information about American geography, natural history, and anthropology of American Indian tribes of the time. "The mind of a scientist with the soul of a poet," John Livingston Lowes. 13 original illustrations, maps. Introduction by Mark Van Doren. 448pp. 5⅜ x 8. T326 Paperbound **$2.00**

STUDIES ON THE STRUCTURE AND DEVELOPMENT OF VERTEBRATES, Edwin Goodrich. The definitive study of the skeleton, fins and limbs, head region, divisions of the body cavity, vascular, respiratory, excretory systems, etc., of vertebrates from fish to higher mammals, by the greatest comparative anatomist of recent times. "The standard textbook," JOURNAL OF ANATOMY. 754 illus. 69-page biographical study. 1186-item bibliography. 2 vols. Total of 906pp. 5⅜ x 8.
Vol. I: S449 Paperbound **$2.50**
Vol. II: S450 Paperbound **$2.50**

THE BIRTH AND DEVELOPMENT OF THE GEOLOGICAL SCIENCES, F. D. Adams. The most complete and thorough history of the earth sciences in print. Covers over 300 geological thinkers and systems; treats fossils, theories of stone growth, paleontology, earthquakes, vulcanists vs. neptunists, odd theories, etc. 91 illustrations, including medieval, Renaissance wood cuts, etc. 632 footnotes and bibliographic notes. 511pp. 308pp. 5⅜ x 8. T5 Paperbound **$2.00**

FROM MAGIC TO SCIENCE, Charles Singer. A close study of aspects of medical science from the Roman Empire through the Renaissance. The sections on early herbals, and "The Visions of Hildegarde of Bingen," are probably the best studies of these subjects available. 158 unusual classic and medieval illustrations. xxvii + 365pp. 5⅜ x 8. T390 Paperbound **$2.00**

SAILING ALONE AROUND THE WORLD, Captain Joshua Slocum. Captain Slocum's personal account of his single-handed voyage around the world in a 34-foot boat he rebuilt himself. A classic of both seamanship and descriptive writing. "A nautical equivalent of Thoreau's account," Van Wyck Brooks. 67 illus. 308pp. 5⅜ x 8. T326 Paperbound **$1.00**

TREES OF THE EASTERN AND CENTRAL UNITED STATES AND CANADA, W. M. Harlow. Standard middle-level guide designed to help you know the characteristics of Eastern trees and identify them at sight by means of an 8-page synoptic key. More than 600 drawings and photographs of twigs, leaves, fruit, other features. xiii + 288pp. 4⅝ x 6½.
T395 Paperbound **$1.35**

FRUIT KEY AND TWIG KEY ("Fruit Key to Northeastern Trees," "Twig Key to Deciduous Woody Plants of Eastern North America"), **W. M. Harlow.** Identify trees in fall, winter, spring. Easy-to-use, synoptic keys, with photographs of every twig and fruit identified. Covers 120 different fruits, 160 different twigs. Over 350 photos. Bibliographies. Glossaries. Total of 143pp. 5⅝ x 8⅜. T511 Paperbound **$1.25**

INTRODUCTION TO THE STUDY OF EXPERIMENTAL MEDICINE, Claude Bernard. This classic records Bernard's far-reaching efforts to transform physiology into an exact science. It covers problems of vivisection, the limits of physiological experiment, hypotheses in medical experimentation, hundreds of others. Many of his own famous experiments on the liver, the pancreas, etc., are used as examples. Foreword by I. B. Cohen. xxv + 266pp. 5⅜ x 8.
T400 Paperbound **$1.50**

THE ORIGIN OF LIFE, A. I. Oparin. The first modern statement that life evolved from complex nitro-carbon compounds, carefully presented according to modern biochemical knowledge of primary colloids, organic molecules, etc. Begins with historical introduction to the problem of the origin of life. Bibliography. xxv + 270pp. 5⅜ x 8. S213 Paperbound **$1.75**

A HISTORY OF ASTRONOMY FROM THALES TO KEPLER, J. L. E. Dreyer. The only work in English which provides a detailed picture of man's cosmological views from Egypt, Babylonia, Greece, and Alexandria to Copernicus, Tycho Brahe and Kepler. "Standard reference on Greek astronomy and the Copernican revolution," SKY AND TELESCOPE. Formerly called "A History of Planetary Systems From Thales to Kepler." Bibliography. 21 diagrams. xvii + 430pp. 5⅜ x 8.
S79 Paperbound **$1.98**

URANIUM PROSPECTING, H. L. Barnes. A professional geologist tells you what you need to know. Hundreds of facts about minerals, tests, detectors, sampling, assays, claiming, developing, government regulations, etc. Glossary of technical terms. Annotated bibliography. x + 117pp. 5⅜ x 8. T309 Paperbound **$1.00**

DE RE METALLICA, Georgius Agricola. All 12 books of this 400 year old classic on metals and metal production, fully annotated, and containing all 289 of the 16th century woodcuts which made the original an artistic masterpiece. A superb gift for geologists, engineers, libraries, artists, historians. Translated by Herbert Hoover & L. H. Hoover. Bibliography, survey of ancient authors. 289 illustrations of the excavating, assaying, smelting, refining, and countless other metal production operations described in the text. 672pp. 6¾ x 10¾. Deluxe library edition. S6 Clothbound **$10.00**

DE MAGNETE, William Gilbert. A landmark of science by the man who first used the word "electricity," distinguished between static electricity and magnetism, and founded a new science. P. F. Mottelay translation. 90 figures. lix + 368pp. 5⅜ x 8. S470 Paperbound **$2.00**

THE AUTOBIOGRAPHY OF CHARLES DARWIN AND SELECTED LETTERS, Francis Darwin, ed. Fascinating documents on Darwin's early life, the voyage of the "Beagle," the discovery of evolution, Darwin's thought on mimicry, plant development, vivisection, evolution, many other subjects Letters to Henslow, Lyell, Hooker, Wallace, Kingsley, etc. Appendix. 365pp. 5⅜ x 8. T479 Paperbound **$1.65**

A WAY OF LIFE AND OTHER SELECTED WRITINGS OF SIR WILLIAM OSLER. 16 of the great physician, teacher and humanist's most inspiring writings on a practical philosophy of life, science and the humanities, and the history of medicine. 5 photographs. Introduction by G. L. Keynes, M.D., F.R.C.S. xx + 278pp. 5⅜ x 8. T488 Paperbound **$1.50**

LITERATURE

WORLD DRAMA, B. H. Clark. 46 plays from Ancient Greece, Rome, to India, China, Japan. Plays by Aeschylus, Sophocles, Euripides, Aristophanes, Plautus, Marlowe, Jonson, Farquhar, Goldsmith, Cervantes, Molière, Dumas, Goethe, Schiller, Ibsen, many others. One of the most comprehensive collections of important plays from all literature available in English. Over 1/3 of this material is unavailable in any other current edition. Reading lists. 2 volumes. Total of 1364pp. 5⅜ x 8. Vol. I, T57 Paperbound **$2.00**
Vol. II, T59 Paperbound **$2.00**

MASTERS OF THE DRAMA, John Gassner. The most comprehensive history of the drama in print. Covers more than 800 dramatists and over 2000 plays from the Greeks to modern Western, Near Eastern, Oriental drama. Plot summaries, theatre history, etc. "Best of its kind in English," NEW REPUBLIC. 35 pages of bibliography. 77 photos and drawings. Deluxe edition. xxii + 890pp. 5⅜ x 8. T100 Clothbound **$5.95**

THE DRAMA OF LUIGI PIRANDELLO, D. Vittorini. All 38 of Pirandello's plays (to 1935) summarized and analyzed in terms of symbolic techniques, plot structure, etc. The only authorized work. Foreword by Pirandello. Biography. Bibliography. xiii + 350pp. 5⅜ x 8.
T435 Paperbound **$1.98**

ARISTOTLE'S THEORY OF POETRY AND THE FINE ARTS, S. H. Butcher, ed. The celebrated "Butcher translation" faced page by page with the Greek text; Butcher's 300-page introduction to Greek poetic, dramatic thought. Modern Aristotelian criticism discussed by John Gassner. lxxvi + 421pp. 5⅜ x 8.
T42 Paperbound **$2.00**

EUGENE O'NEILL: THE MAN AND HIS PLAYS, B. H. Clark. The first published source-book on O'Neill's life and work. Analyzes each play from the early THE WEB up to THE ICEMAN COMETH. Supplies much information about environmental and dramatic influences. ix + 182pp. 5⅜ x 8. T379 Paperbound **$1.25**

INTRODUCTION TO ENGLISH LITERATURE, B. Dobrée, ed. Most compendious literary aid in its price range. Extensive, categorized bibliography (with entries up to 1949) of more than 5,000 poets, dramatists, novelists, as well as historians, philosophers, economists, religious writers, travellers, and scientists of literary stature. Information about manuscripts, important biographical data. Critical, historical, background works not simply listed, but evaluated. Each volume also contains a long introduction to the period it covers.

Vol. I: **THE BEGINNINGS OF ENGLISH LITERATURE TO SKELTON, 1509, W. L. Renwick. H. Orton.** 450pp. 5⅛ x 7⅛. T75 Clothbound **$3.50**

Vol. II: **THE ENGLISH RENAISSANCE, 1510-1688, V. de Sola Pinto.** 381pp. 5⅛ x 7⅛.
T76 Clothbound **$3.50**

Vol. III: **THE AUGUSTANS AND ROMANTICS, 1689-1830, H. Dyson, J. Butt.** 320pp. 5⅛ x 7⅛.
T77 Clothbound **$3.50**

Vol. IV: **THE VICTORIANS AND AFTER, 1830-1914, E. Batho, B. Dobrée.** 360pp. 5⅛ x 7⅛.
T78 Clothbound **$3.50**

EPIC AND ROMANCE, W. P. Ker. The standard survey of Medieval epic and romance by a foremost authority on Medieval literature. Covers historical background, plot, literary analysis, significance of Teutonic epics, Icelandic sagas, Beowulf, French chansons de geste, the Niebelungenlied, Arthurian romances, much more. 422pp. 5⅜ x 8. T355 Paperbound **$1.95**

THE HEART OF EMERSON'S JOURNALS, Bliss Perry, ed. Emerson's most intimate thoughts, impressions, records of conversations with Channing, Hawthorne, Thoreau, etc., carefully chosen from the 10 volumes of The Journals. "The essays do not reveal the power of Emerson's mind . . .as do these hasty and informal writings," N. Y. TIMES. Preface by B. Perry. 370pp. 5⅜ x 8. T447 Paperbound **$1.85**

A SOURCE BOOK IN THEATRICAL HISTORY, A. M. Nagler. (Formerly, "Sources of Theatrical History.") Over 300 selected passages by contemporary observers tell about styles of acting, direction, make-up, scene designing, etc., in the theatre's great periods from ancient Greece to the Théâtre Libre. "Indispensable complement to the study of drama," EDUCATIONAL THEATRE JOURNAL. Prof. Nagler, Yale Univ. School of Drama, also supplies notes, references. 85 illustrations. 611pp. 5⅜ x 8. T515 Paperbound **$2.75**

THE ART OF THE STORY-TELLER, M. L. Shedlock. Regarded as the finest, most helpful book on telling stories to children, by a great story-teller. How to catch, hold, recapture attention; how to choose material; many other aspects. Also includes: a 99-page selection of Miss Shedlock's most successful stories; extensive bibliography of other stories. xxi + 320pp. 5⅜ x 8. T245 Clothbound **$3.50**

THE DEVIL'S DICTIONARY, Ambrose Bierce. Over 1000 short, ironic definitions in alphabetical order, by America's greatest satirist in the classical tradition. "Some of the most gorgeous witticisms in the English language," H. L. Mencken. 144pp. 5⅜ x 8. T487 Paperbound **$1.00**

MUSIC

A DICTIONARY OF HYMNOLOGY, John Julian. More than 30,000 entries on individual hymns, their authorship, textual variations, location of texts, dates and circumstances of composition, denominational and ritual usages, the biographies of more than 9,000 hymn writers, essays on important topics such as children's hymns and Christmas carols, and hundreds of thousands of other important facts about hymns which are virtually impossible to find anywhere else. Convenient alphabetical listing, and a 200-page double-columned index of first lines enable you to track down virtually any hymn ever written. Total of 1786pp. 6¼ x 9¼. 2 volumes. T133. The Set, Clothbound **$15.00**

STRUCTURAL HEARING, TONAL COHERENCE IN MUSIC, Felix Salzer. Extends the well-known Schenker approach to include modern music, music of the middle ages, and Renaissance music. Explores the phenomenon of tonal organization by discussing more than 500 compositions, and offers unusual new insights into the theory of composition and musical relationships. "The foundation on which all teaching in music theory has been based at this college," Leopold Mannes, President, The Mannes College of Music. Total of 658pp. 6½ x 9¼. 2 volumes. S418 The set, Clothbound **$8.00**

A GENERAL HISTORY OF MUSIC, Charles Burney. The complete history of music from the Greeks up to 1789 by the 18th century musical historian who personally knew the great Baroque composers. Covers sacred and secular, vocal and instrumental, operatic and symphonic music; treats theory, notation, forms, instruments; discusses composers, performers, important works. Invaluable as a source of information on the period for students, historians, musicians. "Surprisingly few of Burney's statements have been invalidated by modern research . . . still of great value," NEW YORK TIMES. Edited and corrected by Frank Mercer. 35 figures. 1915pp. 5½ x 8½. 2 volumes. T36 The set, Clothbound **$12.50**

JOHANN SEBASTIAN BACH, Phillip Spitta. Recognized as one of the greatest accomplishments of musical scholarship and far and away the definitive coverage of Bach's works. Hundreds of individual pieces are analyzed. Major works, such as the B Minor Mass and the St. Matthew Passion are examined in minute detail. Spitta also deals with the works of Buxtehude, Pachelbel, and others of the period. Can be read with profit even by those without a knowledge of the technicalities of musical composition. "Unchallenged as the last word on one of the supreme geniuses of music," John Barkham, SATURDAY REVIEW SYNDICATE. Total of 1819pp. 5⅜ x 8. 2 volumes. T252 The set, Clothbound **$10.00**

HISTORY

THE IDEA OF PROGRESS, J. B. Bury. Prof. Bury traces the evolution of a central concept of Western civilization in Greek, Roman, Medieval, and Renaissance thought to its flowering in the 17th and 18th centuries. Introduction by Charles Beard. xl + 357pp. 5⅜ x 8.
T39 Clothbound **$3.95**
T40 Paperbound **$1.95**

THE ANCIENT GREEK HISTORIANS, J. B. Bury. Greek historians such as Herodotus, Thucydides, Xenophon; Roman historians such as Tacitus, Caesar, Livy; scores of others fully analyzed in terms of sources, concepts, influences, etc., by a great scholar and historian. 291pp. 5⅜ x 8. T397 Paperbound **$1.50**

HISTORY OF THE LATER ROMAN EMPIRE, J. B. Bury. The standard work on the Byzantine Empire from 395 A.D. to the death of Justinian in 565 A.D., by the leading Byzantine scholar of our time. Covers political, social, cultural, theological, military history. Quotes contemporary documents extensively. "Most unlikely that it will ever be superseded," Glanville Downey, Dumbarton Oaks Research Library. Genealogical tables. 5 maps. Bibliography. 2 vols. Total of 965pp. 5⅜ x 8. T398, T399 Paperbound, the set **$4.00**

GARDNER'S PHOTOGRAPHIC SKETCH BOOK OF THE CIVIL WAR, Alexander Gardner. One of the rarest and most valuable Civil War photographic collections exactly reproduced for the first time since 1866. Scenes of Manassas, Bull Run, Harper's Ferry, Appomattox, Mechanicsville, Fredericksburg, Gettysburg, etc.; battle ruins, prisons, arsenals, a slave pen, fortifications; Lincoln on the field, officers, men, corpses. By one of the most famous pioneers in documentary photography. Original copies of the "Sketch Book" sold for $425 in 1952. Introduction by E. Bleiler. 100 full-page 7 x 10 photographs (original size). 244pp. 10¾ x 8½
T476 Clothbound **$6.00**

THE WORLD'S GREAT SPEECHES, L. Copeland and L. Lamm, eds. 255 speeches from Pericles to Churchill, Dylan Thomas. Invaluable as a guide to speakers; fascinating as history past and present; a source of much difficult-to-find material. Includes an extensive section of informal and humorous speeches. 3 indices: Topic, Author, Nation. xx + 745pp. 5⅜ x 8.
T468 Paperbound **$2.49**

FOUNDERS OF THE MIDDLE AGES, E. K. Rand. The best non-technical discussion of the transformation of Latin paganism into medieval civilization. Tertullian, Gregory, Jerome, Boethius, Augustine, the Neoplatonists, other crucial figures, philosophies examined. Excellent for the intelligent non-specialist. "Extraordinarily accurate," Richard McKeon, THE NATION. ix + 365pp. 5⅜ x 8. T369 Paperbound **$1.85**

THE POLITICAL THOUGHT OF PLATO AND ARISTOTLE, Ernest Barker. The standard, comprehensive exposition of Greek political thought. Covers every aspect of the "Republic" and the "Politics" as well as minor writings, other philosophers, theorists of the period, and the later history of Greek political thought. Unabridged edition. 584pp. 5⅜ x 8.
T521 Paperbound **$1.85**

PHILOSOPHY

THE GIFT OF LANGUAGE, M. Schlauch. (Formerly, "The Gift of Tongues.") A sound, middle-level treatment of linguistic families, word histories, grammatical processes, semantics, language taboos, word-coining of Joyce, Cummings, Stein, etc. 232 bibliographical notes. 350pp. 5⅜ x 8.
T243 Paperbound **$1.85**

THE PHILOSOPHY OF HEGEL, W. T. Stace. The first work in English to give a complete and connected view of Hegel's entire system. Especially valuable to those who do not have time to study the highly complicated original texts, yet want an accurate presentation by a most reputable scholar of one of the most influential 19th century thinkers. Includes a 14 x 20 fold-out chart of Hegelian system. 536pp. 5⅜ x 8.
T254 Paperbound **$2.00**

ARISTOTLE, A. E. Taylor. A lucid, non-technical account of Aristotle written by a foremost Platonist. Covers life and works; thought on matter, form, causes, logic, God, physics, metaphysics, etc. Bibliography. New index compiled for this edition. 128pp. 5⅜ x 8.
T280 Paperbound **$1.00**

GUIDE TO PHILOSOPHY, C. E. M. Joad. This basic work describes the major philosophic problems and evaluates the answers propounded by great philosophers from the Greeks to Whitehead, Russell. "The finest introduction," BOSTON TRANSCRIPT. Bibliography, 592pp. 5⅜ x 8.
T297 Paperbound **$2.00**

LANGUAGE AND MYTH, E. Cassirer. Cassirer's brilliant demonstration that beneath both language and myth lies an unconscious "grammar" of experience whose categories and canons are not those of logical thought. Introduction and translation by Susanne Langer. Index. x + 103pp. 5⅜ x 8.
T51 Paperbound **$1.25**

SUBSTANCE AND FUNCTION, EINSTEIN'S THEORY OF RELATIVITY, E. Cassirer. This double volume contains the German philosopher's profound philosophical formulation of the differences between traditional logic and the new logic of science. Number, space, energy, relativity, many other topics are treated in detail. Authorized translation by W. C. and M. C. Swabey. xii + 465pp. 5⅜ x 8.
T50 Paperbound **$2.00**

THE PHILOSOPHICAL WORKS OF DESCARTES. The definitive English edition, in two volumes, of all major philosophical works and letters of René Descartes, father of modern philosophy of knowledge and science. Translated by E. S. Haldane and G. Ross. Introductory notes. Total of 842pp. 5⅜ x 8.
T71 Vol. 1, Paperbound **$2.00**
T72 Vol. 2, Paperbound **$2.00**

ESSAYS IN EXPERIMENTAL LOGIC, J. Dewey. Based upon Dewey's theory that knowledge implies a judgment which in turn implies an inquiry, these papers consider such topics as the thought of Bertrand Russell, pragmatism, the logic of values, antecedents of thought, data and meanings. 452pp. 5⅜ x 8.
T73 Paperbound **$1.95**

THE PHILOSOPHY OF HISTORY, G. W. F. Hegel. This classic of Western thought is Hegel's detailed formulation of the thesis that history is not chance but a rational process, the realization of the Spirit of Freedom. Translated and introduced by J. Sibree. Introduction by C. Hegel. Special introduction for this edition by Prof. Carl Friedrich, Harvard University. xxxix + 447pp. 5⅜ x 8.
T112 Paperbound **$1.85**

THE WILL TO BELIEVE and **HUMAN IMMORTALITY, W. James.** Two of James's most profound investigations of human belief in God and immortality, bound as one volume. Both are powerful expressions of James's views on chance vs. determinism, pluralism vs. monism, will and intellect, arguments for survival after death, etc. Two prefaces. 429pp. 5⅜ x 8.
T294 Clothbound **$3.75**
T291 Paperbound **$1.65**

INTRODUCTION TO SYMBOLIC LOGIC, S. Langer. A lucid, general introduction to modern logic, covering forms, classes, the use of symbols, the calculus of propositions, the Boole-Schroeder and the Russell-Whitehead systems, etc. "One of the clearest and simplest introductions," MATHEMATICS GAZETTE. Second, enlarged, revised edition. 368pp. 5⅜ x 8.
S164 Paperbound **$1.75**

MIND AND THE WORLD-ORDER, C. I. Lewis. Building upon the work of Peirce, James, and Dewey, Professor Lewis outlines a theory of knowledge in terms of "conceptual pragmatism," and demonstrates why the traditional understanding of the a priori must be abandoned. Appendices. xiv + 446pp. 5⅜ x 8.
T359 Paperbound **$1.95**

THE GUIDE FOR THE PERPLEXED, M. Maimonides One of the great philosophical works of all time, Maimonides' formulation of the meeting-ground between Old Testament and Aristotelian thought is essential to anyone interested in Jewish, Christian, and Moslem thought in the Middle Ages. 2nd revised edition of the Friedländer translation. Extensive introduction. lix + 414pp. 5⅜ x 8.
T351 Paperbound **$1.85**

THE PHILOSOPHICAL WRITINGS OF PEIRCE, J. Buchler, ed. (Formerly, "The Philosophy of Peirce.") This carefully integrated selection of Peirce's papers is considered the best coverage of the complete thought of one of the greatest philosophers of modern times. Covers Peirce's work on the theory of signs, pragmatism, epistemology, symbolic logic, the scientific method, chance, etc. xvi + 386pp. 5 3/8 x 8. T216 Clothbound **$5.00**
T217 Paperbound **$1.95**

HISTORY OF ANCIENT PHILOSOPHY, W. Windelband. Considered the clearest survey of Greek and Roman philosophy. Examines Thales, Anaximander, Anaximenes, Heraclitus, the Eleatics, Empedocles, the Pythagoreans, the Sophists, Socrates, Democritus, Stoics, Epicureans, Sceptics, Neo-platonists, etc. 50 pages on Plato; 70 on Aristotle. 2nd German edition tr. by H. E. Cushman. xv + 393pp. 5 3/8 x 8. T357 Paperbound **$1.75**

INTRODUCTION TO SYMBOLIC LOGIC AND ITS APPLICATIONS, R. Carnap. A comprehensive, rigorous introduction to modern logic by perhaps its greatest living master. Includes demonstrations of applications in mathematics, physics, biology. "Of the rank of a masterpiece," Z. für Mathematik und ihre Grenzgebiete. Over 300 exercises. xvi + 241pp. 5 3/8 x 8. Clothbound **$4.00**
S453 Paperbound **$1.85**

SCEPTICISM AND ANIMAL FAITH, G. Santayana. Santayana's unusually lucid exposition of the difference between the independent existence of objects and the essence our mind attributes to them, and of the necessity of scepticism as a form of belief and animal faith as a necessary condition of knowledge. Discusses belief, memory, intuition, symbols, etc. xii + 314pp. 5 3/8 x 8. T235 Clothbound **$3.50**
T236 Paperbound **$1.50**

THE ANALYSIS OF MATTER, B. Russell. With his usual brilliance, Russell analyzes physics, causality, scientific inference, Weyl's theory, tensors, invariants, periodicity, etc. in order to discover the basic concepts of scientific thought about matter. "Most thorough treatment of the subject," THE NATION. Introduction. 8 figures. viii + 408pp. 5 3/8 x 8.
T231 Paperbound **$1.95**

THE SENSE OF BEAUTY, G. Santayana. This important philosophical study of why, when, and how beauty appears, and what conditions must be fulfilled, is in itself a revelation of the beauty of language. "It is doubtful if a better treatment of the subject has since appeared," PEABODY JOURNAL. ix + 275pp. 5 3/8 x 8. T238 Paperbound **$1.00**

THE CHIEF WORKS OF SPINOZA. In two volumes. Vol. I: The Theologico-Political Treatise and the Political Treatise. Vol. II: On the Improvement of Understanding, The Ethics, and Selected Letters. The permanent and enduring ideas in these works on God, the universe, religion, society, etc., have had tremendous impact on later philosophical works. Introduction. Total of 862pp. 5 3/8 x 8. T249 Vol. I, Paperbound **$1.50**
T250 Vol. II, Paperbound **$1.50**

TRAGIC SENSE OF LIFE, M. de Unamuno. The acknowledged masterpiece of one of Spain's most influential thinkers. Between the despair at the inevitable death of man and all his works, and the desire for immortality, Unamuno finds a "saving incertitude." Called "a masterpiece," by the ENCYCLOPAEDIA BRITANNICA. xxx + 332pp. 5 3/8 x 8.
T257 Paperbound **$1.95**

EXPERIENCE AND NATURE, John Dewey. The enlarged, revised edition of the Paul Carus lectures (1925). One of Dewey's clearest presentations of the philosophy of empirical naturalism which reestablishes the continuity between "inner" experience and "outer" nature. These lectures are among the most significant ever delivered by an American philosopher. 457pp. 5 3/8 x 8. T471 Paperbound **$1.85**

PHILOSOPHY AND CIVILIZATION IN THE MIDDLE AGES, M. de Wulf. A semi-popular survey of medieval intellectual life, religion, philosophy, science, the arts, etc. that covers feudalism vs. Catholicism, rise of the universities, mendicant orders, and similar topics. Bibliography. viii + 320pp. 5 3/8 x 8. T284 Paperbound **$1.75**

AN INTRODUCTION TO SCHOLASTIC PHILOSOPHY, M. de Wulf. (Formerly, "Scholasticism Old and New.") Prof. de Wulf covers the central scholastic tradition from St. Anselm, Albertus Magnus, Thomas Aquinas, up to Suarez in the 17th century; and then treats the modern revival of. scholasticism, the Louvain position, relations with Kantianism and positivism, etc. xvi + 271pp. 5 3/8 x 8. T296 Clothbound **$3.50**
T283 Paperbound **$1.75**

A HISTORY OF MODERN PHILOSOPHY, H. Höffding. An exceptionally clear and detailed coverage of Western philosophy from the Renaissance to the end of the 19th century. Both major and minor figures are examined in terms of theory of knowledge, logic, cosmology, psychology. Covers Pomponazzi, Bodin, Boehme, Telesius, Bruno, Copernicus, Descartes, Spinoza, Hobbes, Locke, Hume, Kant, Fichte, Schopenhauer, Mill, Spencer, Langer, scores of others. A standard reference work. 2 volumes. Total of 1159pp. 5 3/8 x 8. T117 Vol. 1, Paperbound **$2.00**
T118 Vol. 2, Paperbound **$2.00**

LANGUAGE, TRUTH AND LOGIC, A. J. Ayer. The first full-length development of Logical Posivitism in English. Building on the work of Schlick, Russell, Carnap, and the Vienna school, Ayer presents the tenets of one of the most important systems of modern philosophical thought. 160pp. 5 3/8 x 8. T10 Paperbound **$1.25**

ORIENTALIA AND RELIGION

THE MYSTERIES OF MITHRA, F. Cumont. The great Belgian scholar's definitive study of the Persian mystery religion that almost vanquished Christianity in the ideological struggle for the Roman Empire. A masterpiece of scholarly detection that reconstructs secret doctrines, organization, rites. Mithraic art is discussed and analyzed. 70 illus. 239pp. 5⅜ x 8.
T323 Paperbound **$1.85**

CHRISTIAN AND ORIENTAL PHILOSOPHY OF ART. A. K. Coomaraswamy. The late art historian and orientalist discusses artistic symbolism, the role of traditional culture in enriching art, medieval art, folklore, philosophy of art, other similar topics. Bibliography. 148pp. 5⅜ x 8.
T378 Paperbound **$1.25**

TRANSFORMATION OF NATURE IN ART, A. K. Coomaraswamy. A basic work on Asiatic religious art. Includes discussions of religious art in Asia and Medieval Europe (exemplified by Meister Eckhart), the origin and use of images in Indian art, Indian Medieval aesthetic manuals, and other fascinating, little known topics. Glossaries of Sanskrit and Chinese terms. Bibliography. 41pp. of notes. 245pp. 5⅜ x 8. T368 Paperbound **$1.75**

ORIENTAL RELIGIONS IN ROMAN PAGANISM, F. Cumont. This well-known study treats the ecstatic cults of Syria and Phrygia (Cybele, Attis, Adonis, their orgies and mutilatory rites); the mysteries of Egypt (Serapis, Isis, Osiris); Persian dualism; Mithraic cults; Hermes Trismegistus, Ishtar, Astarte, etc. and their influence on the religious thought of the Roman Empire. Introduction. 55pp. of notes; extensive bibliography. xxiv + 298pp. 5⅜ x 8.
T321 Paperbound **$1.75**

ANTHROPOLOGY, SOCIOLOGY, AND PSYCHOLOGY

PRIMITIVE MAN AS PHILOSOPHER, P. Radin. A standard anthropological work based on Radin's investigations of the Winnebago, Maori, Batak, Zuni, other primitive tribes. Describes primitive thought on the purpose of life, marital relations, death, personality, gods, etc. Extensive selections of original primitive documents. Bibliography. xviii + 420pp. 5⅜ x 8.
T392 Paperbound **$2.00**

PRIMITIVE RELIGION, P. Radin. Radin's thoroughgoing treatment of supernatural beliefs, shamanism, initiations, religious expression, etc. in primitive societies. Arunta, Ashanti, Aztec, Bushman, Crow, Fijian, many other tribes examined. "Excellent," NATURE. New preface by the author. Bibliographic notes. x + 322pp. 5⅜ x 8. T393 Paperbound **$1.85**

SEX IN PSYCHO-ANALYSIS, S. Ferenczi. (Formerly, "Contributions to Psycho-analysis.") 14 selected papers on impotence, transference, analysis and children, dreams, obscene words, homosexuality, paranoia, etc. by an associate of Freud. Also included: THE DEVELOPMENT OF PSYCHO-ANALYSIS, by Ferenczi and Otto Rank. Two books bound as one. Total of 406pp. 5⅜ x 8. T324 Paperbound **$1.85**

THE PRINCIPLES OF PSYCHOLOGY, William James. The complete text of the famous "long course," one of the great books of Western thought. An almost incredible amount of information about psychological processes, the stream of consciousness, habit, time perception, memory, emotions, reason, consciousness of self, abnormal phenomena, and similar topics. Based on James's own discoveries integrated with the work of Descartes, Locke, Hume, Royce, Wundt, Berkeley, Lotse, Herbart, scores of others. "A classic of interpretation," PSYCHIATRIC QUARTERLY. 94 illus. 1408pp. 2 volumes. 5⅜ x 8.
T381 Vol. 1, Paperbound **$2.50**
T382 Vol. 2, Paperbound **$2.50**

THE POLISH PEASANT IN EUROPE AND AMERICA, W. I. Thomas, F. Znaniecki. Monumental sociological study of peasant primary groups (family and community) and the disruptions produced by a new industrial system and emigration to America, by two of the foremost sociologists of recent times. One of the most important works in sociological thought. Includes hundreds of pages of primary documentation; point by point analysis of causes of social decay, breakdown of morality, crime, drunkenness, prostitution, etc. 2nd revised edition. 2 volumes. Total of 2250pp. 6 x 9. T478 2 volume set, Clothbound **$12.50**

FOLKWAYS, W. G. Sumner. The great Yale sociologist's detailed exposition of thousands of social, sexual, and religious customs in hundreds of cultures from ancient Greece to Modern Western societies. Preface by A. G. Keller. Introduction by William Lyon Phelps. 705pp. 5⅜ x 8. S508 Paperbound **$2.49**

BEYOND PSYCHOLOGY, Otto Rank. The author, an early associate of Freud, uses psychoanalytic techniques of myth-analysis to explore ultimates of human existence. Treats love, immortality, the soul, sexual identity, kingship, sources of state power, many other topics which illuminate the irrational basis of human existence. 291pp. 5⅜ x 8. T485 Paperbound **$1.75**

ILLUSIONS AND DELUSIONS OF THE SUPERNATURAL AND THE OCCULT, D. H. Rawcliffe. A rational, scientific examination of crystal gazing, automatic writing, table turning, stigmata, the Indian rope trick, dowsing, telepathy, clairvoyance, ghosts, ESP, PK, thousands of other supposedly occult phenomena. Originally titled "The Psychology of the Occult." 14 illustrations. 551pp. 5⅜ x 8. T503 Paperbound **$2.00**

YOGA: A SCIENTIFIC EVALUATION, Kovoor T. Behanan. A scientific study of the physiological and psychological effects of Yoga discipline, written under the auspices of the Yale University Institute of Human Relations. Foreword by W. A. Miles, Yale Univ. 17 photographs. 290pp. 5⅜ x 8. T505 Paperbound **$1.65**

HOAXES, C. D. MacDougall. Delightful, entertaining, yet scholarly exposition of how hoaxes start, why they succeed, documented with stories of hundreds of the most famous hoaxes. "A stupendous collection . . . and shrewd analysis, "NEW YORKER. New, revised edition. 54 photographs. 320pp. 5⅜ x 8. T465 Paperbound **$1.75**

CREATIVE POWER: THE EDUCATION OF YOUTH IN THE CREATIVE ARTS, Hughes Mearns. Named by the National Education Association as one of the 20 foremost books on education in recent times. Tells how to help children express themselves in drama, poetry, music, art, develop latent creative power. Should be read by every parent, teacher. New, enlarged, revised edition. Introduction. 272pp. 5⅜ x 8. T490 Paperbound **$1.50**

LANGUAGES

NEW RUSSIAN-ENGLISH, ENGLISH-RUSSIAN DICTIONARY, M. A. O'Brien. Over 70,000 entries in new orthography! Idiomatic usages, colloquialisms. One of the few dictionaries that indicate accent changes in conjugation and declension. "One of the best," Prof. E. J. Simmons, Cornell. First names, geographical terms, bibliography, many other features. 738pp. 4½ x 6¼. T208 Paperbound **$2.00**

MONEY CONVERTER AND TIPPING GUIDE FOR EUROPEAN TRAVEL, C. Vomacka. Invaluable, handy source of currency regulations, conversion tables, tipping rules, postal rates, much other travel information for every European country plus Israel, Egypt and Turkey. 128pp. 3½ x 5¼. T260 Paperbound **60¢**

MONEY CONVERTER AND TIPPING GUIDE FOR TRAVEL IN THE AMERICAS (including the United States and Canada), **C. Vomacka.** The information you need for informed and confident travel in the Americas: money conversion tables, tipping guide, postal, telephone rates, etc. 128pp. 3½ x 5¼. T261 Paperbound **65¢**

DUTCH-ENGLISH, ENGLISH-DUTCH DICTIONARY, F. G. Renier. The most convenient, practical Dutch-English dictionary on the market. New orthography. More than 60,000 entries: idioms, compounds, technical terms, etc. Gender of nouns indicated. xviii + 571pp. 5½ x 6¼. T224 Clothbound **$2.50**

LEARN DUTCH!, F. G. Renier. The most satisfactory and easily-used grammar of modern Dutch. Used and recommended by the Fulbright Committee in the Netherlands. Over 1200 simple exercises lead to mastery of spoken and written Dutch. Dutch-English, English-Dutch vocabularies. 181pp. 4¼ x 7¼. T441 Clothbound **$1.75**

PHRASE AND SENTENCE DICTIONARY OF SPOKEN RUSSIAN, English-Russian, Russian-English. Based on phrases and complete sentences, rather than isolated words; recognized as one of the best methods of learning the idiomatic speech of a country. Over 11,500 entries, indexed by single words, with more than 32,000 English and Russian sentences and phrases, in immediately usable form. Probably the largest list ever published. Shows accent changes in conjugation and declension; irregular forms listed in both alphabetical place and under main form of word. 15,000 word introduction covering Russian sounds, writing, grammar, syntax. 15-page appendix of geographical names, money, important signs, given names, foods, special Soviet terms, etc. Travellers, businessmen, students, government employees have found this their best source for Russian expressions. Originally published as U.S. Government Technical Manual TM 30-944. iv + 573pp. 5⅝ x 8⅜. T496 Paperbound **$2.75**

PHRASE AND SENTENCE DICTIONARY OF SPOKEN SPANISH, Spanish-English, English-Spanish. Compiled from spoken Spanish, emphasizing idiom and colloquial usage in both Castilian and Latin-American. More than 16,000 entries containing over 25,000 idioms—the largest list of idiomatic constructions ever published. Complete sentences given, indexed under single words —language in immediately usable form, for travellers, businessmen, students, etc. 25-page introduction provides rapid survey of sounds, grammar, syntax, with full consideration of irregular verbs. Especially apt in modern treatment of phrases and structure. 17-page glossary gives translations of geographical names, money values, numbers, national holidays, important street signs, useful expressions of high frequency, plus unique 7-page glossary of Spanish and Spanish-American foods and dishes. Originally published as U.S. Government Technical Manual TM 30-900. iv + 513pp. 5⅝ x 8⅜. T495 Paperbound **$1.75**

SAY IT language phrase books

"SAY IT" in the foreign language of your choice! We have sold over ½ million copies of these popular, useful language books. They will not make you an expert linguist overnight, but they do cover most practical matters of everyday life abroad.

Over 1000 useful phrases, expressions, with additional variants, substitutions.

Modern! Useful! Hundreds of phrases not available in other texts: "Nylon," "air-conditioned," etc.

The ONLY inexpensive phrase book **completely indexed.** Everything is available at a flip of your finger, ready for use.

Prepared by native linguists, travel experts.

Based on years of travel experience abroad.

This handy phrase book may be used by itself, or it may supplement any other text or course; it provides a living element. Used by many colleges and institutions: Hunter College; Barnard College; Army Ordnance School, Aberdeen; and many others.

Available, 1 book per language:

Danish (T818) 75¢
Dutch T(817) 75¢
English (for German-speaking people) (T801) 60¢
English (for Italian-speaking people) (T816) 60¢
English (for Spanish-speaking people) (T802) 60¢
Esperanto (T820) 75¢
French (T803) 60¢
German (T804) 60¢
Modern Greek (T813) 75¢
Hebrew (T805) 60¢
Italian (T806) 60¢
Japanese (T807) 60¢
Norwegian (T814) 75¢
Russian (T810) 75¢
Spanish (T811) 60¢
Turkish (T821) 75¢
Yiddish (T815) 75¢
Swedish (T812) 75¢
Polish (T808) 75¢
Portuguese (T809) 75¢

LISTEN & LEARN language record sets

LISTEN & LEARN is the only language record course designed especially to meet your travel needs, or help you learn essential foreign language quickly by yourself, or in conjunction with any school course, by means of the automatic association method. Each set contains three 33⅓ rpm long-playing records — 1½ hours of recorded speech by eminent native speakers who are professors at Columbia, N.Y.U., Queens College and other leading universities. The sets are priced far below other sets of similar quality, yet they contain many special features not found in other record sets:

* Over 800 selected phrases and sentences, a basic vocabulary of over 3200 words.
* Both English and foreign language recorded; with a pause for your repetition.
* Designed for persons with limited time; no time wasted on material you cannot use immediately.
* Living, modern expressions that answer modern needs: drugstore items, "air-conditioned," etc.
* 128-196 page manuals contain everything on the records, plus simple pronunciation guides.
* Manual is fully indexed; find the phrase you want instantly.
* High fidelity recording—equal to any records costing up to $6 each.

The phrases on these records cover 41 different categories useful to the traveller or student interested in learning the living, spoken language: greetings, introductions, making yourself understood, passing customs, planes, trains, boats, buses, taxis, nightclubs, restaurants, menu items, sports, concerts, cameras, automobile travel, repairs, drugstores, doctors, dentists, medicines, barber shops, beauty parlors, laundries, many, many more.

"Excellent . . . among the very best on the market," Prof. Mario Pei, Dept. of Romance Languages, Columbia University. "Inexpensive and well-done . . . an ideal present," CHICAGO SUNDAY TRIBUNE. "More genuinely helpful than anything of its kind which I have previously encountered," Sidney Clark, well-known author of "ALL THE BEST" travel books. Each set contains 3 33⅓ rpm pure vinyl records, 128- 196 page with full record text, and album. One language per set. LISTEN & LEARN record sets are now available in—

FRENCH	the set $4.95	**GERMAN**	the set $4.95
ITALIAN	the set $4.95	**SPANISH**	the set $4.95
RUSSIAN	the set $5.95	**JAPANESE** *	the set $5.95

* Available Sept. 1, 1959

UNCONDITIONAL GUARANTEE: Dover Publications stands behind every Listen and Learn record set. If you are dissatisfied with these sets for any reason whatever, return them within 10 days and your money will be refunded in full.

ART HISTORY

STICKS AND STONES, Lewis Mumford. An examination of forces influencing American architecture: the medieval tradition in early New England, the classical influence in Jefferson's time, the Brown Decades, the imperial facade, the machine age, etc. "A truly remarkable book," SAT. REV. OF LITERATURE. 2nd revised edition. 21 illus. xvii + 228pp. 5⅜ x 8.
T202 Paperbound **$1.60**

THE AUTOBIOGRAPHY OF AN IDEA, Louis Sullivan. The architect whom Frank Lloyd Wright called "the master," records the development of the theories that revolutionized America's skyline. 34 full-page plates of Sullivan's finest work. New introduction by R. M. Line. xiv + 335pp. 5⅜ x 8.
T281 Paperbound **$1.85**

THE MATERIALS AND TECHNIQUES OF MEDIEVAL PAINTING, D. V. Thompson. An invaluable study of carriers and grounds, binding media, pigments, metals used in painting, al fresco and al secco techniques, burnishing, etc. used by the medieval masters. Preface by Bernard Berenson. 239pp. 5⅜ x 8.
T327 Paperbound **$1.85**

PRINCIPLES OF ART HISTORY, H. Wölfflin. This remarkably instructive work demonstrates the tremendous change in artistic conception from the 14th to the 18th centuries, by analyzing 164 works by Botticelli, Dürer, Hobbema, Holbein, Hals, Titian, Rembrandt, Vermeer, etc., and pointing out exactly what is meant by "baroque," "classic," "primitive," "picturesque," and other basic terms of art history and criticism. "A remarkable lesson in the art of seeing," SAT. REV. OF LITERATURE. Translated from the 7th German edition. 150 illus. 254pp. 6⅛ x 9¼.
T276 Paperbound **$2.00**

FOUNDATIONS OF MODERN ART, A. Ozenfant. Stimulating discussion of human creativity from paleolithic cave painting to modern painting, architecture, decorative arts. Fully illustrated with works of Gris, Lipchitz, Leger, Picasso, primitive, modern artifacts, architecture, industrial art, much more. 226 illustrations. 368pp. 6⅛ x 9¼.
T215 Paperbound **$1.95**

HANDICRAFTS, APPLIED ART, ART SOURCES, ETC.

WILD FOWL DECOYS, J. Barber. The standard work on this fascinating branch of folk art, ranging from Indian mud and grass devices to realistic wooden decoys. Discusses styles, types, periods; gives full information on how to make decoys. 140 illustrations (including 14 new plates) show decoys and provide full sets of plans for handicrafters, artists, hunters, and students of folk art. 281pp. 7⅞ x 10¾. Deluxe edition.
T11 Clothbound **$8.50**

METALWORK AND ENAMELLING, H. Maryon. Probably the best book ever written on the subject. Tells everything necessary for the home manufacture of jewelry, rings, ear pendants, bowls, etc. Covers materials, tools, soldering, filigree, setting stones, raising patterns, repoussé work, damascening, niello, cloisonné, polishing, assaying, casting, and dozens of other techniques. The best substitute for apprenticeship to a master metalworker. 363 photos and figures. 374pp. 5½ x 8½.
T183 Clothbound **$7.50**

SHAKER FURNITURE, E. D. and F. Andrews. The most illuminating study of Shaker furniture ever written. Covers chronology, craftsmanship, houses, shops, etc. Includes over 200 photographs of chairs, tables, clocks, beds, benches, etc. "Mr. & Mrs. Andrews know all there is to know about Shaker furniture," Mark Van Doren, NATION. 48 full-page plates. 192pp. Deluxe cloth binding. 7⅞ x 10¾.
T7 Clothbound **$6.00**

PRIMITIVE ART, Franz Boas. A great American anthropologist covers theory, technical virtuosity, styles, symbolism, patterns, etc. of primitive art. The more than 900 illustrations will interest artists, designers, craftworkers. Over 900 illustrations. 376pp. 5⅜ x 8.
T25 Paperbound **$1.95**

ON THE LAWS OF JAPANESE PAINTING, H. Bowie. The best possible substitute for lessons from an oriental master. Treats both spirit and technique; exercises for control of the brush; inks, brushes, colors; use of dots, lines to express whole moods, etc. 220 illus. 132pp. 6⅛ x 9¼.
T30 Paperbound **$1.95**

HANDBOOK OF ORNAMENT, F. S. Meyer. One of the largest collections of copyright-free traditional art: over 3300 line cuts of Greek, Roman, Medieval, Renaissance, Baroque, 18th and 19th century art motifs (tracery, geometric elements, flower and animal motifs, etc.) and decorated objects (chairs, thrones, weapons, vases, jewelry, armor, etc.). Full text. 3300 illustrations. 562pp. 5⅜ x 8.
T302 Paperbound **$2.00**

THREE CLASSICS OF ITALIAN CALLIGRAPHY. Oscar Ogg, ed. Exact reproductions of three famous Renaissance calligraphic works: Arrighi's OPERINA and IL MODO, Tagliente's LO PRESENTE LIBRO, and Palatino's LIBRO NUOVO. More than 200 complete alphabets, thousands of lettered specimens, in Papal Chancery and other beautiful, ornate handwriting. Introduction. 245 plates. 282pp. 6⅛ x 9¼.
T212 Paperbound **$1.95**

THE HISTORY AND TECHNIQUES OF LETTERING, A. Nesbitt. A thorough history of lettering from the ancient Egyptians to the present, and a 65-page course in lettering for artists. Every major development in lettering history is illustrated by a complete alphabet. Fully analyzes such masters as Caslon, Koch, Garamont, Jenson, and many more. 89 alphabets, 165 other specimens. 317pp. 5⅜ x 8.
T427 Paperbound **$2.00**

LETTERING AND ALPHABETS, J. A. Cavanagh. An unabridged reissue of "Lettering," containing the full discussion, analysis, illustration of 89 basic hand lettering tyles based on Caslon, Bodoni, Gothic, many other types. Hundreds of technical hints on construction, strokes, pens, brushes, etc. 89 alphabets, 72 lettered specimens, which may be reproduced permission-free. 121pp. 9¾ x 8. T53 Paperbound **$1.25**

THE HUMAN FIGURE IN MOTION, Eadweard Muybridge. The largest collection in print of Muybridge's famous high-speed action photos. 4789 photographs in more than 500 action-strip-sequences (at shutter speeds up to 1/6000th of a second) illustrate men, women, children—mostly undraped—performing such actions as walking, running, getting up, lying down, carrying objects, throwing, etc. "An unparalleled dictionary of action for all artists," AMERICAN ARTIST. 390 full-page plates, with 4789 photographs. Heavy glossy stock, reinforced binding with headbands. 7⅞ x 10¾. T204 Clothbound **$10.00**

ANIMALS IN MOTION, Eadweard Muybridge. The largest collection of animal action photos in print. 34 different animals (horses, mules, oxen, goats, camels, pigs, cats, lions, gnus, deer, monkeys, eagles—and 22 others) in 132 characteristic actions. All 3919 photographs are taken in series at speeds up to 1/1600th of a second, offering artists, biologists, cartoonists a remarkable opportunity to see exactly how an ostrich's head bobs when running, how a lion puts his foot down, how an elephant's knee bends, how a bird flaps his wings, thousands of other hard-to-catch details. "A really marvelous series of plates," NATURE. 380 full-pages of plates. Heavy glossy stock, reinforced binding with headbands. 7⅞ x 10¾. T203 Clothbound **$10.00**

THE BOOK OF SIGNS, R. Koch. 493 symbols—crosses, monograms, astrological, biological symbols, runes, etc.—from ancient manuscripts, cathedrals, coins, catacombs, pottery. May be reproduced permission-free. 493 illustrations by Fritz Kredel. 104pp. 6⅛ x 9¼. T162 Paperbound **$1.00**

A HANDBOOK OF EARLY ADVERTISING ART, C. P. Hornung. The largest collection of copyright-free early advertising art ever compiled. Vol. I: 2,000 illustrations of animals, old automobiles, buildings, allegorical figures, fire engines, Indians, ships, trains, more than 33 other categories! Vol II: Over 4,000 typographical specimens; 600 Roman, Gothic, Barnum, Old English faces; 630 ornamental type faces; hundreds of scrolls, initials, flourishes, etc. "A remarkable collection," PRINTERS' INK.

Vol. I: Pictorial Volume. Over 2000 illustrations. 256pp. 9 x 12. T122 Clothbound **$10.00**
Vol. II: Typographical Volume. Over 4000 speciments. 319pp. 9 x 12. T123 Clothbound **$10.00**
Two volume set, Clothbound, only **$18.50**

DESIGN FOR ARTISTS AND CRAFTSMEN, L. Wolchonok. The most thorough course on the creation of art motifs and designs. Shows you step-by-step, with hundreds of examples and 113 detailed exercises, how to create original designs from geometric patterns, plants, birds, animals, humans, and man-made objects. "A great contribution to the field of design and crafts," N. Y. SOCIETY OF CRAFTSMEN. More than 1300 entirely new illustrations. xv + 207pp. 7⅞ x 10¾. T274 Clothbound **$4.95**

HANDBOOK OF DESIGNS AND DEVICES, C. P. Hornung. A remarkable working collection of 1836 basic designs and variations, all copyright-free. Variations of circle, line, cross, diamond, swastika, star, scroll, shield, many more. Notes on symbolism. "A necessity to every designer who would be original without having to labor heavily," ARTIST and ADVERTISER. 204 plates. 240pp. 5⅜ x 8. T125 Paperbound **$1.90**

THE UNIVERSAL PENMAN, George Bickham. Exact reproduction of beautiful 18th century book of handwriting. 22 complete alphabets in finest English roundhand, other scripts, over 2000 elaborate flourishes, 122 calligraphic illustrations, etc. Material is copyright-free. "An essential part of any art library, and a book of permanent value," AMERICAN ARTIST. 212 plates. 224pp. 9 x 13¾. T20 Clothbound **$10.00**

AN ATLAS OF ANATOMY FOR ARTISTS, F. Schider. This standard work contains 189 full-page plates, more than 647 illustrations of all aspects of the human skeleton, musculature, cutaway portions of the body, each part of the anatomy, hand forms, eyelids, breasts, location of muscles under the flesh, etc. 59 plates illustrate how Michelangelo, da Vinci, Goya, 15 others, drew human anatomy. New 3rd edition enlarged by 52 new illustrations by Cloquet, Barcsay. "The standard reference tool," AMERICAN LIBRARY ASSOCIATION. "Excellent," AMERICAN ARTIST. 189 plates, 647 illustrations. xxvi + 192pp. 7⅞ x 10⅝. T241 Clothbound **$6.00**

AN ATLAS OF ANIMAL ANATOMY FOR ARTISTS, W. Ellenberger, H. Baum, H. Dittrich. The largest, richest animal anatomy for artists in English. Form, musculature, tendons, bone structure, expression, detailed cross sections of head, other features, of the horse, lion, dog, cat, deer, seal, kangaroo, cow, bull, goat, monkey, hare, many other animals. "Highly recommended," DESIGN. Second, revised, enlarged edition with new plates from Cuvier, Stubbs, etc. 288 illustrations. 153pp. 11⅜ x 9. T82 Clothbound **$6.00**

ANIMAL DRAWING: ANATOMY AND ACTION FOR ARTISTS, C. R. Knight. 158 studies, with full accompanying text, of such animals as the gorilla, bear, bison, dromedary, camel, vulture, pelican, iguana, shark, etc., by one of the greatest modern masters of animal drawing. Innumerable tips on how to get life expression into your work. "An excellent reference work,' SAN FRANCISCO CHRONICLE. 158 illustrations. 156pp. 10½ x 8½. T426 Paperbound **$2.00**

DOVER BOOKS

THE CRAFTSMAN'S HANDBOOK, Cennino Cennini. The finest English translation of IL LIBRO DELL' ARTE, the 15th century introduction to art technique that is both a mirror of Quatrocento life and a source of many useful but nearly forgotten facets of the painter's art. 4 illustrations. xxvii + 142pp. D. V. Thompson, translator. 6⅛ x 9¼. T54 Paperbound **$1.50**

THE BROWN DECADES, Lewis Mumford. A picture of the "buried renaissance" of the post-Civil War period, and the founding of modern architecture (Sullivan, Richardson, Root, Roebling), landscape development (Marsh, Olmstead, Eliot), and the graphic arts (Homer, Eakins, Ryder). 2nd revised, enlarged edition. Bibliography. 12 illustrations. xiv + 266 pp. 5⅜ x 8. T200 Paperbound **$1.65**

STIEGEL GLASS, F. W. Hunter. The story of the most highly esteemed early American glassware, fully illustrated. How a German adventurer, "Baron" Stiegel, founded a glass empire; detailed accounts of individual glasswork. "This pioneer work is reprinted in an edition even more beautiful than the original," ANTIQUES DEALER. New introduction by Helen McKearin. 171 illustrations, 12 in full color. xxii + 338pp. 7⅞ x 10¾. T128 Clothbound **$10.00**

THE HUMAN FIGURE, J. H. Vanderpoel. Not just a picture book, but a complete course by a famous figure artist. Extensive text, illustrated by 430 pencil and charcoal drawings of both male and female anatomy. 2nd enlarged edition. Foreword. 430 illus. 143pp. 6⅛ x 9¼. T432 Paperbound **$1.45**

PINE FURNITURE OF EARLY NEW ENGLAND, R. H. Kettell. Over 400 illustrations, over 50 working drawings of early New England chairs, benches, beds cupboards, mirrors, shelves, tables, other furniture esteemed for simple beauty and character. "Rich store of illustrations . . . emphasizes the individuality and varied design," ANTIQUES. 413 illustrations, 55 working drawings. 475pp. 8 x 10¾. T145 Clothbound **$10.00**

BASIC BOOKBINDING, A. W. Lewis. Enables both beginners and experts to rebind old books or bind paperbacks in hard covers. Treats materials, tools; gives step-by-step instruction in how to collate a book, sew it, back it, make boards, etc. 261 illus. Appendices. 155pp. 5⅜ x 8. T169 Paperbound **$1.35**

DESIGN MOTIFS OF ANCIENT MEXICO, J. Enciso. Nearly 90% of these 766 superb designs from Aztec, Olmec, Totonac, Maya, and Toltec origins are unobtainable elsewhere! Contains plumed serpents, wind gods, animals, demons, dancers, monsters, etc. Excellent applied design source. Originally $17.50. 766 illustrations, thousands of motifs. 192pp. 6⅛ x 9¼. T84 Paperbound **$1.85**

AFRICAN SCULPTURE, Ladislas Segy. 163 full-page plates illustrating masks, fertility figures, ceremonial objects, etc., of 50 West and Central African tribes—95% never before illustrated. 34-page introduction to African sculpture. "Mr. Segy is one of its top authorities," NEW YORKER. 164 full-page photographic plates. Introduction. Bibliography. 244pp. 6⅛ x 9¼. T396 Paperbound **$2.00**

THE PROCESSES OF GRAPHIC REPRODUCTION IN PRINTING, H. Curwen. A thorough and practical survey of wood, linoleum, and rubber engraving; copper engraving; drypoint, mezzotint, etching, aquatint, steel engraving, die sinking, stencilling, lithography (extensively); photographic reproduction utilizing line, continuous tone, photoengravure, collotype; every other process in general use. Note on color reproduction. Section on bookbinding. Over 200 illustrations, 25 in color. 143pp. 5½ x 8½. T512 Clothbound **$4.00**

CALLIGRAPHY, J. G. Schwandner. First reprinting in 200 years of this legendary book of beautiful handwriting. Over 300 ornamental initials, 12 complete calligraphic alphabets, over 150 ornate frames and panels, 75 calligraphic pictures of cherubs, stags, lions, etc., thousands of flourishes, scrolls, etc., by the greatest 18th century masters. All material can be copied or adapted without permission. Historical introduction. 158 full-page plates. 368pp. 9 x 13. T475 Clothbound **$10.00**

* * *

A DIDEROT PICTORIAL ENCYCLOPEDIA OF TRADES AND INDUSTRY, Manufacturing and the Technical Arts in Plates Selected from "L'Encyclopédie ou Dictionnaire Raisonné des Sciences, des Arts, et des Métiers," of Denis Diderot, edited with text by C. Gillispie. Over 2000 illustrations on 485 full-page plates. Magnificent 18th century engravings of men, women, and children working at such trades as milling flour, cheesemaking, charcoal burning, mining, silverplating, shoeing horses, making fine glass, printing, hundreds more, showing details of machinery, different steps in sequence, etc. A remarkable art work, but also the largest collection of working figures in print, copyright-free, for art directors, designers, etc. Two vols. 920pp. 9 x 12. Heavy library cloth. T421 Two volume set **$18.50**

* * *

SILK SCREEN TECHNIQUES, J. Biegeleisen, M. Cohn. A practical step-by-step home course in one of the most versatile, least expensive graphic arts processes. How to build an inexpensive silk screen, prepare stencils, print, achieve special textures, use color, etc. Every step explained, diagrammed. 149 illustrations, 8 in color. 201pp. 6⅛ x 9¼. T433 Paperbound **$1.45**

CATALOG OF

PUZZLES, GAMES, AND ENTERTAINMENTS

MATHEMATICS, MAGIC AND MYSTERY, Martin Gardner. Astonishing feats of mind reading, mystifying "magic" tricks, are often based on mathematical principles anyone can learn. This book shows you how to perform scores of tricks with cards, dice, coins, knots, numbers, etc., by using simple principles from set theory, theory of numbers, topology, other areas of mathematics, fascinating in themselves. No special knowledge required. 135 illus. 186pp. 5⅜ x 8.
T335 Paperbound **$1.00**

MATHEMATICAL PUZZLES FOR BEGINNERS AND ENTHUSIASTS, G. Mott-Smoth. Test your problem-solving techniques and powers of inference on 188 challenging, amusing puzzles based on algebra, dissection of plane figures, permutations, probabilities, etc. Appendix of primes, square roots, etc. 135 illus. 2nd revised edition. 248pp. 5⅜ x 8.
T198 Paperbound **$1.00**

LEARN CHESS FROM THE MASTERS, F. Reinfeld. Play 10 games against Marshall, Bronstein, Najdorf, other masters, and grade yourself on each move. Detailed annotations reveal principles of play, strategy, etc. as you proceed. An excellent way to get a real insight into the game. Formerly titled, "Chess by Yourself." 91 diagrams. vii + 144pp. 5⅜ x 8.
T362 Paperbound **$1.00**

REINFELD ON THE END GAME IN CHESS, F. Reinfeld. 62 end games of Alekhine, Tarrasch, Morphy, other masters, are carefully analyzed with emphasis on transition from middle game to end play. Tempo moves, queen endings, weak squares, other basic principles clearly illustrated. Excellent for understanding why some moves are weak or incorrect, how to avoid errors. Formerly titled, "Practical End-game Play." 62 diagrams. vi + 177pp. 5⅜ x 8.
T417 Paperbound **$1.25**

101 PUZZLES IN THOUGHT AND LOGIC, C. R. Wylie, Jr. Brand new puzzles you need no special knowledge to solve! Each one is a gem of ingenuity that will really challenge your problem-solving technique. Introduction with simplified explanation of scientic puzzle solving. 128pp. 5⅜ x 8.
T167 Paperbound **$1.00**

THE COMPLETE NONSENSE OF EDWARD LEAR. The only complete edition of this master of gentle madness at a popular price. The Dong with the Luminous Nose, The Jumblies, The Owl and the Pussycat, hundreds of other bits of wonderful nonsense. 214 limericks, 3 sets of Nonsense Botany, 5 Nonsense Alphabets, 546 fantastic drawings, much more. 320pp. 5⅜ x 8.
T167 Paperbound **$1.00**

28 SCIENCE FICTION STORIES OF H. G. WELLS. Two complete novels, "Men Like Gods" and "Star Begotten," plus 26 short stories by the master science-fiction writer of all time. Stories of space, time, future adventure that are among the all-time classics of science fiction. 928pp. 5⅜ x 8.
T265 Clothbound **$3.95**

SEVEN SCIENCE FICTION NOVELS, H. G. Wells. Unabridged texts of "The Time Machine," "The Island of Dr. Moreau," "First Men in the Moon," "The Invisible Man," "The War of the Worlds," "The Food of the Gods," "In the Days of the Comet." "One will have to go far to match this for entertainment, excitement, and sheer pleasure," N. Y. TIMES. 1015pp. 5⅜ x 8.
T264 Clothbound **$3.95**

MATHEMAGIC, MAGIC PUZZLES, AND GAMES WITH NUMBERS, R. V. Heath. More than 60 new puzzles and stunts based on number properties: multiplying large numbers mentally, finding the date of any day in the year, etc. Edited by J. S. Meyer. 76 illus. 129pp. 5⅜ x 8.
T110 Paperbound **$1.00**

FIVE ADVENTURE NOVELS OF H. RIDER HAGGARD. The master story-teller's five best tales of mystery and adventure set against authentic African backgrounds: "She," "King Solomon's Mines," "Allan Quatermain," "Allan's Wife," "Maiwa's Revenge." 821pp. 5⅜ x 8.
T108 Clothbound **$3.95**

WIN AT CHECKERS, M. Hopper. (Formerly "Checkers.") The former World's Unrestricted Checker Champion gives you valuable lessons in openings, traps, end games, ways to draw when you are behind, etc. More than 100 questions and answers anticipate your problems. Appendix. 75 problems diagrammed, solved. 79 figures. xi + 107pp. 5⅜ x 8.
T363 Paperbound **$1.00**

CRYPTOGRAPHY, L. D. Smith. Excellent introductory work on ciphers and their solution, history of secret writing, techniques, etc. Appendices on Japanese methods, the Baconian cipher, frequency tables. Bibliography. Over 150 problems, solutions. 160pp. 5⅜ x 8.
T247 Paperbound **$1.00**

CRYPTANALYSIS, H. F. Gaines. (Formerly, "Elementary Cryptanalysis.") The best book available on cryptograms and how to solve them. Contains all major techniques: substitution, transposition, mixed alphabets, multafid, Kasiski and Vignere methods, etc. Word frequency appendix. 167 problems, solutions. 173 figures. 236pp. 5⅜ x 8.
T97 Paperbound **$1.95**

FLATLAND, E. A. Abbot. The science-fiction classic of life in a 2-dimensional world that is considered a first-rate introduction to relativity and hyperspace, as well as a scathing satire on society, politics and religion. 7th edition. 16 illus. 128pp. 5⅜ x 8.
T1 Paperbound **$1.00**